BALANCING ENVIRONMENTAL, SOCIAL, AND GOVERNANCE GOALS

WHAT BANKS AND COMPANIES CAN DO ON ESG AND SUSTAINABILITY

WALID R. ALAMEDDIN

ARCHWAY
PUBLISHING

This book is a work of non-fiction. Unless otherwise noted, the author and the publisher make no explicit guarantees as to the accuracy of the information contained in this book and in some cases, names of people and places have been altered to protect their privacy.

Archway Publishing books may be ordered through booksellers or by contacting:

Archway Publishing
1663 Liberty Drive
Bloomington, IN 47403
www.archwaypublishing.com
844-669-3957

Because of the dynamic nature of the Internet, any web addresses or links contained in this book may have changed since publication and may no longer be valid. The views expressed in this work are solely those of the author and do not necessarily reflect the views of the publisher, and the publisher hereby disclaims any responsibility for them.

Any people depicted in stock imagery provided by Getty Images are models, and such images are being used for illustrative purposes only. Certain stock imagery © Getty Images.

ISBN: 978-1-6657-2010-6 (sc)
ISBN: 978-1-6657-2009-0 (hc)
ISBN: 978-1-6657-2011-3 (e)

Library of Congress Control Number: 2022908337

Print information available on the last page.

Archway Publishing rev. date: 5/7/2022

CONTENTS

INTRODUCTION

WHY THIS BOOK?

We in Amdeya were surprised when we saw the results of the survey we conducted on 701 banks in forty-one emerging countries. Only 32 percent of the surveyed banks had reporting on Environmental, Social, and Governance goals (known as ESG goals). Sixty-eight percent of these banks made no mention of ESG at all in their disclosures. The survey was conducted in 2020 and 2021 and also showed that many of the banks that reported on ESG have started to do that only recently.

We had initiated the survey to see how much ESG is taking hold on the ground in emerging countries. What the survey shows is that there is clearly a major gap in implementing, even planning, ESG programs among companies and banks in emerging countries. There is obviously a lot of work that needs to be done. This book is meant to help accelerate the needed efforts to have ESG become a mainstream activity in all banks and companies in emerging countries.

This book serves as a guide of what is included in Environmental, Social and Governance goals. It also, and equally importantly, covers why certain goals are included in ESG. The book explains why each of the main ESG goals is needed and demonstrates that there would be an impact from the actions to be taken to implement the selected ESG goals. Moreover, and in addition to showing what ESG actions are needed, and why they are needed, this book will cover how banks and companies worldwide can pursue and implement ESG goals and programs. Finally, the book will provide detailed guidelines of the ESG information that needs to be reported.

This book will help professionals in banks and companies to set ESG objectives, pursue them, implement them, and keep developing them. Moreover, it can serve as the academic book for a course on Environmental, Social and Governance goals because it covers the main elements of ESG in a scientific, methodical way.

The book will have more focus on banks and companies in the emerging and developing countries who need a somewhat different approach to ESG than banks in developed countries.

We will also show in this book that ESG goals are achievable and that it is in the interest of the banks and companies in the emerging countries to have ESG goals and pursue them.

Environmental, Social, and Governance considerations, or ESG, have been gaining major importance among investors, companies, banks, and policy makers in the last decade. These nonfinancial-management considerations are developing fast in developed economies. They are also starting to be important in the emerging countries. The trend to include ESG factors in business is progressing in parallel with a similar global movement by governments to pursue these goals. The latter has been best reflected in the United Nation's Sustainable Development Goals (SDGs), which were set in 2015.

Most banks and companies can certainly do more in the Environmental, Social and Governance areas. Nowhere is this truer than in the emerging countries. This is reflected in the Amdeya survey of 701 banks globally, which found that less than one-third of those banks report on ESG as mentioned earlier.

The emerging countries also lag the developed countries in this regard, with some countries not having a single bank reporting on ESG. The banks that have ESG reports in the emerging countries are also mostly the larger banks in those countries.

The Amdeya ESG survey, however, shows that the number of banks reporting on ESG has been increasing each year, and this trend is expected to continue. The Amdeya ESG survey shows that almost half the banks surveyed plan to report on ESG in three years, and most are likely to have ESG reports in five years.

This book will provide guidelines to facilitate the disclosure and reporting of ESG activities, mainly by banks, financial institutions, and companies in emerging countries. This is in addition to providing guidelines of how to set ESG goals and pursue them, as mentioned earlier. Good reporting would help ensure that the ESG measures being reported are themselves effective. Moreover, it will become clear that these reports need to be verified to ensure that they are credible. We will devote a chapter to what ESG indicators need to be reported. We will devote another chapter to how independent verification of ESG reporting is to be carried out.

Many banks and companies that do not report on ESG already cover many of the elements of ESG. They just need to plan these better, make them more comprehensive, and report on them. It would not take a major effort for them to report on ESG as the larger banks in the emerging markets are already doing.

Moreover, many regulators globally have started to demand that their banks and companies report on some elements of ESG and on verification of ESG "labeling" of financial products and ESG bank reports. We will devote a chapter on what regulators are doing on ESG.

After covering why this book is needed, we will cover what this book will include.

WHAT DOES ESG INCLUDE?

ESG, as is well-known, stands for Environmental, Social and Governance goals. Sustainability is a similar concept, except that sustainability generally includes more focus on economic factors and less on governance. ESG is now the more generally accepted term for these activities. We will use the terms *ESG* and *sustainability* to mean the same thing in this book.

The general impression, which is not correct, is that ESG focuses mostly on environmental factors and that climate change is what is meant by environmental. Environmental goals actually include other important elements. Most important among environmental elements, in addition to the most important one covering climate change, are water availability and quality, air pollution, plastic reduction, and waste management. These factors are as critical, especially in emerging countries, as climate change is.

Social, the second pillar of ESG, includes many elements and goals that are very important in the emerging countries. These include education, health, financial inclusion, and gender (female) equality, among others we will discuss later in this book.

Governance, the third pillar of ESG, is already being given special attention by banks worldwide. Most regulators have extensive requirements for good governance among the banks they regulate. However, the effectiveness of governance in many banks is generally not independently verified.

This book will discuss each of the three pillars of ESG in detail. One chapter will cover the main elements of environmental goals as they relate to climate change. Another chapter will cover environmental goals that are not directly related to climate change, such as water availability. A third chapter will cover the main elements of social goals. A fourth chapter will cover the guidelines of good governance. Simple measurements of each element will be chosen to help banks and companies manage them.

We have outlined why there is a need for this book and the main areas it covers. We will now describe in broad terms the balanced approach we believe banks and companies should follow in setting and pursuing ESG goals.

A BALANCED APPROACH TO ACHIEVING
ENVIRONMENTAL, SOCIAL, AND GOVERNANCE GOALS

We will devote a full chapter of this book to make the case that banks and companies, especially in emerging countries, need to have a balanced approach in pursuing ESG goals.

We will show that a balanced approach to ESG is the most effective and most suitable approach to implement ESG by banks and companies in the emerging countries. We believe the call for a balanced approach to ESG would incentivize banks and companies in the emerging countries to fully engage in the global ESG efforts.

It is important to define what we mean by a "balanced approach" to achieve ESG goals. We will do this in detail in a separate chapter, but it is worthwhile to give at the outset the broad outline of what is involved in this approach.

A balanced approach to ESG should first recognize that addressing climate change is the most important goal among ESG goals.

Yet a balanced approach also means that the selected ESG objectives should be comprehensive and include elements from all three broad goals of ESG. The need to balance and take into account all environmental, social, and governance considerations when setting objectives and implementing them reflects the diversity of interests of the many stakeholders of a bank or a company. These stakeholders include investors, shareholders, clients, employees, suppliers, international financial institutions, rating agencies, and regulators.

The fact that banks and companies can approach ESG as a balanced package that includes Environmental, Social, and Governance goals would allow them to choose what is more material to the companies, based on their own criteria. There is less imposition of certain goals, and there is more freedom of choice of goals.

Moreover, a balanced approach means that banks can be selective of the main objectives/goals they choose to pursue. The selected objectives would be ones that are material, relevant, practical, and implementable and have the highest impact for the stakeholders and community each bank serves. This is what is meant by the "materiality" principle.

A balanced approach by banks should also take into consideration the impact from the activities they finance and not only from their own activities. A balanced approach would have the banks factor into their ESG plans the environmental and social activities they finance—and governance they ask for from their clients.

To properly set environmental goals, a balanced approach to ESG takes into consideration the different elements of these environmental (E) goals. These include addressing, in addition to tackling climate change, the issues of water scarcity and cleanliness, air quality, pollution of the seas, and waste management, among others.

A balanced approach would moreover allow some emerging countries to focus on the non-environmental elements of ESG, specifically social and governance goals. The return on investment in social and/or governance would be higher than their investment in E for some of these countries.

The business aspects of ESG should also be taken into consideration in a balanced approach. To ensure ESG becomes embedded in the business of a company or bank, it is important that ESG should not be seen as a "cost center." To the extent possible, there should be revenues associated with ESG activities. These revenues would include financing alternative energy (solar, wind, …), financing health businesses, education, women's owned business, and all activities that would help meet ESG targets.

A balanced approach to ESG recognizes finally that there will be a transition phase until ESG goals are met. This is because all realistic scenarios indicate that many of the environmental, social and even governance indicators will remain unacceptable, or get worse, in the next few years, before they (hopefully) are made to improve.

Before going into the next chapters of this book, it is worthwhile outlining in this introduction why it is important for banks in the emerging countries to pursue ESG goals. We would then discuss how the lack of common ESG standards and regulatory guidelines have been reasons why some banks have not engaged yet in ESG activities, but why they should take action on ESG anyway. This would include the fact ESG is now good for business. We would finally outline the "Target Operating ESG Model for Banks" as it has been developing.

THE ROLE OF EMERGING MARKETS BANKS IN ACHIEVING ESG GOALS

It is important for banks in the emerging countries to have ESG goals and pursue them because banks in the emerging and developing countries can have a very impactful role in achieving ESG goals in their countries.

There are several reasons that enable banks in emerging markets to play a central role in achieving ESG goals in their economies. The following are the main factors and considerations that lead to this conclusion.

1. Banks in the Emerging Markets have generally a major role in their economies. The relative size of banks to GDP tends to be around 1:1 in many of these economies. These medium and small sized banks happen to be major players, in relative terms, in many of the economies they are based in.
2. The capital markets in emerging markets are still generally much smaller in size than the banking sector. The corporations also tend to be smaller than banks. The role that corporations would be expected to take in ESG would therefore be smaller than that of banks, and less than corporations in more developed economies.
3. The fact banks in the emerging countries play a major role in their emerging market economies means that they have the capability of playing a major role (and sometimes the major role) in achieving ESG goals in their countries.
4. The attention on the progress of emerging markets in ESG appears to be secondary among major global investment firms. This is understandable given the relatively small size of these

economies. This means the domestic banks have to do their ESG homework themselves, and rely only marginally on outside investors in ESG. This is notwithstanding that well-managed ESG projects in the emerging countries should continue to target international investors as they bring "fresh" money, which would have higher marginal returns than "local" money.

5. The emerging markets can leverage the global interest in improving the environment, to attract assistance from developed countries to achieve their countries' Social and Governance goals, as well as the Environmental ones. This would be assistance from the governments (as the main investment firms are less focused on the emerging markets as mentioned in the above point). Part of this assistance can be channeled through the emerging markets banks where it can be most effectively used.

6. The banks in emerging markets have the most developed management and information systems relative to most other players in these economies. This would enable them to pursue ESG targets, and help measure progress of these elements in their economies.

7. Banks in the emerging markets are generally closer to their governments than they might be in the developed economies. This is because they have a more dominant role relative to their economies than their global counterparts. This in turn means that these banks can coordinate their ESG programs with the ESG plans of the public sector. Many necessary ESG activities can also become more achievable, and doable, for profit-making banks if these banks are given incentives by their governments.

THE DEVELOPING COMMON INTERNATIONAL ESG STANDARDS AND REGULATORY GUIDELINES FOR BANKS

One major reason there have been delays in ESG reporting by most banks globally is that there are no generally accepted common international standards for measurement of ESG.

Several international bodies have been working towards reaching common ESG standards and common measurements. These would be ESG standards that apply to all companies in all industries, including the financial industry. These basically aim at one-size-fits-all standards. Other more targeted standards aim at particular elements of ESG, most notably climate-change. Yet none of these published standards have gained overall acceptance, especially in the financial industry. The standard setting efforts remain work-in-progress. Regulators have also not yet come to agreement on common ESG regulatory guidelines, partly because there are no common standards.

Many of the more serious ESG standardization efforts, and the more comprehensive ones, are aimed at large corporations, and large banks. These are rational and impactful efforts, because the most significant ESG work can be done by the largest corporations and banks.

The large global banks have been reporting on ESG using one or more of the available standards. Bank of America gets the prize for reporting, for it had several ESG reports in 2019. Each of these reports followed one of the well-known standards. It has consolidated its ESG reporting in 2020.

It is clear that banks in the emerging markets have challenges following all these standards, because they do not have the resources of a Bank of America. Moreover, comprehensive reporting according to these different standards is not necessarily very relevant to medium and small banks that make up almost all the banks in the emerging markets. This is one reason why many banks in the emerging markets do not report on ESG, as the Amdeya ESG survey of more than 700 banks in emerging markets has shown.

Most banks, especially smaller banks, find the current standards too comprehensive and complicated. It is worth noting that most of the banks in the emerging markets have assets less than $100 billion, and very few of these banks have assets above $300 billion.

Moreover, the lack of common ESG standards, especially those targeted at smaller banks and companies, also explains why even the banks that do report on ESG in the emerging markets have challenges in their ESG reporting. Many of these reports appear perfunctory as a result of these challenges.

Moreover, regulators, especially banking regulators, have not yet come up with regulations related to ESG reporting. We will devote a chapter of this book to the regulatory initiatives and standards governing ESG.

BANKS AND COMPANIES NEED TO WORK ON ACHIEVING ESG GOALS WITHOUT WAITING FOR AGREEMENT ON INTERNATIONAL STANDARDS AND REGULATORY GUIDELINES

It is clear that one-size-fits-all standards are not a good fit for all companies, including banks. The standards that exist are not all pertinent to the banking business. This is because the existing standards are mostly targeted at investors in all sectors, particularly those that pursue impact investing.

Moreover, because they are also aimed at large corporations, medium and small companies and banks find it unwieldy to implement these standards in full.

Yet banks and companies should not wait for the common ESG standards and measurements to be agreed upon. Banks everywhere, including in the emerging markets, need to have ESG objectives and plans, implement them, and disclose these to their many stakeholders. This is because bank stakeholders want to see that their banks are pursuing ESG goals. These stakeholders include investors, shareholders, clients, employees, suppliers, international financial institutions, rating agencies, and regulators.

If banks, and Emerging Economies, are to attract international investors, they need to be seen as meeting measurable Environmental, Social and Governance targets. The goal is to move on, as large banks are doing. No bank will have perfect measurements and reporting. Doing a partial job is better than doing nothing.

Reporting on ESG is certainly necessary. The non-reporting of what a company, or a bank is doing on ESG would increasingly be seen as possible absence of any action (or interest) in ESG. It could be seen eventually as "non-compliant" when more ESG guidelines are issued by regulators.

Separate, stand-alone ESG/sustainability reports are also necessary. Some companies and banks now report on ESG in a section of their annual reports, and this reporting tends to be perfunctory. Stand-alone ESG reports help bring focus on ESG issues.

This ESG reporting should also not be a one-size-fits-all. This is because some companies and banks have different business profiles, different sizes, and different impact on the economies they serve. What is "material" to the stakeholders of one bank might not be material to other banks. Moreover, it is for each bank, and each country to determine their objectives in the ESG spheres, especially in Social and Governance spheres. We will devote a full chapter to what ESG indicators banks and companies can report on.

It should also be understood that reporting on ESG is reporting on the progress of ESG implementation. ESG goals are themselves not short-term goals, and are expected to be achieved in the medium to long term. This applies to almost all elements of ESG. Net-zero emissions, for example, are expected to be achieved in 2050. Obviously any reporting on this goal is a progress report by the very nature of the activity being reported on. The same would apply to other goals, like gender equality. So whether a bank or a company is reporting on ESG activities for the first time, or in the fifth year, its reports are progress reports. This would also be progress reporting on the transition of ESG activities from basic ones to more comprehensive ones. Moreover, reporting itself would also be expected to improve with time, as common standards become more widely acceptable, and as data becomes more available.

ESG IS GOOD FOR BUSINESS

Banks are recognizing that it is rewarding, and profitable, to be active in the ESG space. The track record now clearly shows that investments with high ESG scores, have generally better financial returns in the medium and long run than standard investments. International investors are also demanding that the investments they participate in take into consideration ESG factors because of expected higher returns, and because many are becoming more sensitive to ESG considerations. This is generally called impact investing. Moreover, banks that are seen as ESG-aware are more likely in the future to attract relationships with investors and global banks, than ones who are not seen as paying attention to ESG.

Environmentally friendly activities, like financing alternative energy, can be profitable. Moreover, socially friendly investments, like micro finance, education lending, and health lending, can all be profitable if their related risks are well-managed. All the risks that banks face can certainly be well managed with strong governance, the third pillar of ESG.

In all cases, it is important for any ESG program to make sense from a business point of view. Unprofitable activities, ESG or otherwise, cannot be sustainable. Marginally profitable ESG activities can possibly be encouraged by incentives from the public sector to make them more attractive to investors and banks.

There is also an "intangible" value that comes from pursuing ESG goals. This comes from being seen as, and being, "socially responsible." The Corporate Social Responsibility (CSR) criteria, which preceded ESG, have been pursued for years by many banks and companies worldwide. Moreover, banks who already pursue "ethical banking" would find it smooth sailing from ethical banking into the wider seas of ESG.

The future trends point clearly that banks in the emerging markets need to give increasing attention to ESG in their business. It is highly likely that the more successful banks would be those that factor in ESG now in their plans, and report on these in a structured manner, on an annual verifiable basis.

THE TARGET OPERATING ESG MODEL FOR BANKS

The operating ESG model that we see developing for most banks in the next few years, including in emerging markets, is the following:

1. Banks would have ESG objectives and plans
2. Banks would have selected ESG metrics
3. Banks would implement their ESG plans
4. Banks monitor their own progress on achieving their ESG objectives
5. Banks monitor (and measure) the ESG activities of their clients
6. Banks disclose their ESG activities in annual stand-alone reports
7. Banks get independent assurance/verification of their ESG reports
8. Rating agencies factor-in ESG reporting in their rating of a bank or a company they rate.
9. Regulators provide ESG guidelines to Banks, and Financial Institutions.
10. Regulators monitor compliance of Banks and Financial Institutions with ESG guidelines.

What we are proposing in this book is for medium and small sized banks to follow ESG standards and goals, which they can measure, and would be able to manage. These are goals and measurements that they can select from the existing more complex and more comprehensive ones. This would follow the proportionality principles of Basel, which stipulate that what is expected of a bank or financial institution would be commensurate with its size.

The selected goals and metrics for medium or small sized banks, especially those in the emerging markets, would also follow the "balanced approach" we have already mentioned. They would include all the material components of Environmental, Social and Governance goals, but in a more simplified form. These selected metrics will be given in a separate chapter, which would also reflect the need for a balanced approach.

Our goal is to have practical, implementable guidelines. The ESG objectives and outcomes need to be measurable, to the extent possible. However, if specific measurements cannot be made of a certain objective, action should still be taken and continued to achieve the "general" objective.

This book will follow ESG in the order it has come to be commonly used. We would first go over Environmental factors and goals, then Social, then Governance goals.

1

ENVIRONMENTAL GOALS: CLIMATE CHANGE

INTRODUCTION

ALL COUNTRIES ARE FACING MAJOR environmental issues that need to be addressed, and where investments to address them can have significant impact.

We will divide environmental issues into two broad categories in this book, and cover them in two different chapters. The first is climate change, and its related activities. The second includes the other environmental factors, most important among which are water availability and sanitation, and air quality.

It would become clear in the two chapters on environmental goals that many emerging countries need to have a balance between the focus on climate change, and the focus on other environmental issues which might be more pressing. The need for balance among environmental issues is in addition to the need to have an overall balance between environmental, social and governance goals.

The stakeholders of a bank, or a company, increasingly want environmental factors to be taken into consideration in the activities of the bank they deal with. International investors, and large international banks would increasingly be asking, and expecting the smaller banks in the emerging markets to advise them on what they are doing about environmental goals. This is because the larger banks are themselves being asked to report on what they are doing about environmental goals. The smaller banks are basically "clients" of the large international banks, and banks are expected to ensure their clients take into consideration the concerns of their stakeholders.

The main environmental issues that need to be tackled, and which will be covered in this and the next chapter, relate to both climate change, and other issues that are not necessarily all directly related to climate change. We will start with climate change in this chapter.

CLIMATE CHANGE

Climate change is the main environmental issue globally that needs to be addressed. It is also in many developing countries the main ESG goal to have. It refers mostly to the global warming that has been witnessed over the last few decades, and which is getting worse. The increases in weather temperatures have been witnessed across the globe, and with several countries registering their hottest years on record in the last ten years.

The fact global warming is happening is borne out by the record. Globally, according to NASA's GISS (Goddard Institute for Space Studies), the last 7 years have been the warmest on record. This is based on readings from 26,000 weather stations worldwide. Several countries have had record weather temperatures as well. France, which has one of the best historical records, has had the hottest seven years in the last 120 years in the last ten years. Similarly, in Germany 2018 witnessed the highest temperatures on record, with 2020 a close second. The U.S., which has 126 year national temperature records, the five warmest years have all occurred since 2012. India, which has temperature records since 1901, the five hottest years were all in the last 12 years, with 2016 being the hottest.

Global warming has adverse effects in most countries. Draughts have increased in frequency and intensity. Extreme weather conditions have also increased. The intensity and frequency of hurricanes have increased.

Deserts have been steadily replacing arable lands. Sea water levels have been rising, as ice caps have been melting away. Climate change is having, and will increasingly have, severe economic effects across the globe.

Some studies suggest that "irreversibility" would occur if temperatures rise between 2.2 to 4 degrees centigrade (4 to 7.2 Fahrenheit) above the temperatures of the preindustrial "base" level (before 1900). Extinction levels could possibly start to happen if temperatures rise further 5 to 6 degrees (9-10.8 F) above the "base" level.

The causes of climate change can all be traced to human activities. Increasing populations, and improvements in their economic conditions all require more food, and energy.

Economic growth due to both population growth, and increasing per capita incomes, is highly correlated with activities that emit greenhouse gases, or GHGs. These gases cause global warming in the same way that temperatures rise in a greenhouse. These gases block some of the heat generated by economic activities from escaping out of earth's atmosphere. Moreover, GHGs block some of the heat that comes from the sun from escaping as well. Furthermore, the fact ice is melting away reduces the sun's heat that is reflected by the ice. All three factors cause heat to be trapped in the atmosphere, and earth's temperature to rise.

Environmental adverse changes present, in the views of many, the most important challenges facing the livelihood of all countries in the coming years. Global warming in particular is occurring, by its very nature, in all countries, and is not hampered by political borders. Tackling global environmental challenges needs therefore to be a collective global effort.

The efforts to address this global challenge are now global. Every country is now involved in these efforts. Businesses, banks, and individuals are taking, or expected to take important roles in these efforts.

Each country, however, needs to carry a burden according to its capability. Each bank or company would also be expected to do its share, even if it is relatively small. The Banking industry, and individual banks, need to increasingly factor in elements brought about by climate change and global warming in their lending and other activities.

The efforts to address climate change focus on addressing GHGs emissions. These efforts are complex because the activities that produce GHGs are varied, and inter-connected. We will cover in this chapter first what these GHGs are, then go over the needed developments in the energy industry to address climate change, as this industry is the main producer of GHGs. We will also cover the efforts to capture carbon dioxide and other GHGs. We will put these in the global framework to address climate change, which is the Paris Accord. We will finally sum up what companies and banks, especially in the emerging markets, can do about climate change.

GHGS

<u>What are Greenhouse Gases:</u>

The greenhouse gases that are generated by human controlled activities are mainly Carbon Dioxide, Methane, Nitrous Oxide, and F-gases. As carbon dioxide (carbon for short) is the dominant GHG gas, all other emissions are measured in carbon dioxide equivalent. The measurement unit used is metric ton of carbon dioxide equivalent. Equivalent is defined as having the same warming effect as carbon dioxide over a period of 100 years. This is the metric adopted by the UNFCCC (The United Nations Framework Convention on Climate Change).

Different GHG's have a) different impacts on climate warming, and b) each of these GHG's remains present for different durations in the atmosphere.

The formula to convert GHG's into carbon dioxide equivalent is simple: it is the mass of a gas, times its global warming potential (GWP). The GWP measures the warming impact compared to carbon, over a 100 year period.

It should be noted that all the non-carbon GHG gases have a higher GWP than carbon. Methane has a factor of 28, and Nitrous Oxide a factor of 265.

However, the total emissions are dominated by carbon dioxide, as they constitute almost 75% of the total GHG emissions globally. It is followed by Methane (17%) Nitrous Oxide (6%), and F-gases (2%). The latter include hydrofluorocarbons (HFCs), and sulfur hexafluoride (SF6). These numbers are from 2019 according to the World Resources Institute and other sources. The data is all in carbon dioxide equivalent. The global emission of GHGs is estimated at 50 gigatons in 2020.

Carbon dioxide is emitted mostly by fossil fuels. Removal of forests (deforestation) can also increase carbon dioxide. Methane (CH_4) is produced by agricultural activities (including raising cattle), waste management, and biomass burning. Nitrous oxide (N_2O) is produced mostly by fertilizer usage. And F gases are generated mostly by refrigeration and other industrial processes.

Measuring GHG Emissions:

Emissions of carbon dioxide and carbon dioxide equivalents are measured in tons, usually metric tons (1000 kilogram). Larger measurements include million tons, and gigatons (Gt, which is one billion tons).

Another measurement of carbon dioxide is how much of it remains in the atmosphere. The metric used is parts per million (ppm). Carbon dioxide levels were 270 ppm (parts per million) in 1980. In 2019 they reached 414 ppm. Some may think that these volumes are relatively small. The point is that these relatively small amounts do have large effects on heating the globe. Carbon dioxide is also a direct cause of increasing water vapor, which is far larger than carbon dioxide in the atmosphere, and can have a large role in preventing the earth's heat from escaping into space. This 414 ppm level existed only 3 million years ago, when temperatures were 2-3 degrees centigrade above pre-industrial temperatures, and the seas were 15-25 meters (50-80 feet) higher than today. However, there were several other factors that caused the changes in these pre-historic times, and carbon dioxide atmospheric concentrations might have been a result (rather than a cause) of these other factors/determinants.

There are different methods to measure the GHGs at the business level. A generally used terminology is that by the Greenhouse Gas Protocol. There are three scopes of GHG emissions according to this methodology:

Scope 1 Emissions: These are direct emissions from the activities of a company or a bank, or under their control. These include emissions from the company's offices and vehicles.

Scope 2 Emissions: These are indirect emissions mainly from electricity purchased by the company or bank.

Scope 3 Emissions: These are indirect emissions from the activities of a company or a bank that are generated by sources that they do not own or control. These are more complex to measure than Scope 1 and Scope 2 emissions.

Scope 3 emissions, according to the Protocol, include "all indirect emissions (not included in Scope 2) that occur in the value chain of the reporting company, including both upstream and downstream emissions." Upstream emissions are indirect emissions related to "purchased" goods and services. Downstream emissions, on the other hand, include indirect emissions related to "sold" goods and services. There are 15 categories of emissions, of which 8 are upstream, and 7 are downstream.

One of the best examples we can find about Scope 3 emission reductions is what the U.S. retail giant Walmart is doing. Walmart has found out that around 90% of its total emissions (Scopes 1, 2, and 3) come from Scope 3 from its own suppliers. Walmart has accordingly agreed with 3100 of its suppliers to work on reducing their GHG emissions – by up to one gigaton, or one billion tons of carbon dioxide equivalent. This would be a permanent reduction, and certainly a remarkable one given that global emissions annually amount to 50 gigatons.

Reporting scope 3 emissions would likely result in double counting, because the emissions reported are emissions of other entities. Those other entities might themselves report these emissions, or a third party that uses these products might itself also report them.

There are however particular issues for banks and financial institutions in how Scope 3 emissions are measured. This is because the main Scope 3 emissions the banks have are generated by their clients who the banks lend to. The emissions by a bank's clients (all Scope 3) can obviously be far larger than the emissions of the bank (Scope 1 and Scope 2).

Banks, including in the emerging markets, would find that the Scope 3 emissions of their clients are significant, especially compared to the bank's own emissions. They would need accordingly to try to measure them and/or have their clients measure them. They would then need them to be disclosed.

There are several efforts to address this issue, and among these is the "standard" issued in early 2021 by the PCAF (Partnership for Carbon Accounting Financials). The PCAF has developed GHG accounts and reporting standards of Scope 3 emissions particularly for the financial industry. It provides guidelines to measure (and then disclose) GHG emissions associated with six asset classes. These are a) listed equity and corporate bonds, b) business loans and unlisted equity, c) project finance, d) commercial real estate, d) mortgages, and e) motor vehicle loans.

Another Scope 3 calculation methodology can be found in the "Corporate Value Chain (Scope 3) Accounting and Reporting Standard," which is a supplement of the "GHG Protocol Corporate Accounting and Reporting Standard."

Regulators might find that their banks are ideally suited to measure and report the emissions of a significant part of the economy. This is because most entities that have major emissions are clients of banks (e.g., cement, or agriculture companies). The banks are also well suited to do that because they have the systems and human resources to undertake these tasks – possibly more than the public sector, or the clients of the banks themselves.

The Assurance (or verification) process of Scope 3 emissions is also more complex. This would be carried out by independent third parties, as we would see in the chapter on Assurance. The assurance would most likely be "limited" (involving a negative statement, such as "not aware that the reporting is not accurate"). It would be difficult to have the more comprehensive, "reasonable" assurance (involving a positive opinion, such as "reporting reflects fairly," etc.).

A company, or a bank, in an emerging country should report Scope

1 and Scope 2 emissions. There is no need to report Scope 3 emissions at initial stages/years of reporting (mainly because of the difficulty of collecting data). However, Scope 3 emissions of banks (reflected mainly in loans) would likely become a major area of GHG measurement and disclosure of their emissions in the next few years. The sooner banks can start collecting data on these emissions, the easier it would be to disclose them in later years.

Achieving Carbon Neutrality and Net-Zero:

It is necessary at this point to introduce the concepts of "carbon neutrality," and "net zero."

Carbon Neutrality is defined as the point where all carbon emissions from an entity are balanced by carbon removed by the entity. If carbon removal cannot be made, then an entity can achieve carbon neutrality by offsetting its emissions. These offsets can be achieved by purchasing carbon credits from an entity that has carbon negative (or climate positive) activities, such as a solar or wind-powered plant. Carbon Neutrality covers mostly Scope 1 and Scope 2 emissions.

To reach carbon neutrality, an entity (a company or a bank) should first calculate its carbon emissions. This is called the Carbon Footprint, which is total greenhouse gas emissions by a person, organization, event, or product. The company/bank should then put a plan to reduce these, and/or purchase or finance carbon negative activities (or carbon credits).

Net-zero is a broader concept. It is when an entity (or a country) has an incremental addition of zero to GHGs. According to a 2019 paper by the Science Based Targets initiative (SBTi), Net Zero is defined as "achieving a state in which the activities within the value-chain of an organization result in no net impact on the climate from greenhouse gas emissions." This does not take into consideration the already existing GHGs in the atmosphere, which have been increasing exponentially over the last decades.

The Paris Accord aims to achieve net-zero by 2050 for the planet as a whole. We will briefly cover the Paris Accord in a separate section of this chapter.

A country, company, or a bank, can achieve net zero if it removes emissions equal to what it produces. It can alternatively do that by producing energy only from non-carbon-emitting methods. Net Zero covers Scope 1, Scope 2, and Scope 3 emissions

To achieve net zero, greenhouse gas removals (GGR) are almost always needed. On the other hand, to achieve carbon neutrality, it would be sufficient for one organization to acquire (or purchase) carbon offsets.

Carbon offsets are "purchased" in units of metric tons of carbon dioxide, or carbon dioxide equivalent. Carbon offsets are brought about, according to the GHG Protocol from "activities intended to reduce GHG emissions, increase the storage of carbon, or enhance GHG removals from the atmosphere." Offsets can be used to "neutralize" Scope 1 and 2 emissions. Some argue that offsets can be used to neutralize Scope 3 emissions as well (but only for a company/bank, but not a country). There are several standards to measure carbon neutrality. One of the better ones is PAS 2060, the carbon neutral standard developed by BSI (the British Standards Institute).

A "related" program used in some countries to achieve neutrality is the REC: Renewable Energy Certificate. RECs are tradable instruments, and can be only used to "neutralize" Scope 2 emissions. Their sources are specifically renewable energy generators (e.g. wind, or solar power). The units that measure RECs are Megawatt hours (MWh), unlike the metric tons carbon dioxide equivalent of offset programs.

Sources of Greenhouse Gases: GHGs

One way that is commonly used to look at how GHGs are produced is to break down the activities that produce them. We will give below two of the categorizations of these activities. The first is the more commonly used one by the IPCC (Intergovernmental Panel on Climate Change), and the second is aggregated by Bill Gates (which is possibly a more "user-friendly" categorization).

The IPCC categorization of global GHG emissions, as also given by the EIA (the U.S. Energy Information Administration), was as follows for the most recent year of reporting:

1.	Electricity and Heat Production	25%
2.	Other Energy	10%
3.	Agriculture	24%
4.	Transportation	14%
5.	Industry	21%
6.	Buildings	6%
	TOTAL	**100%**

A different categorization of the same GHG sources given by Bill Gates in his 2021 book on climate change is as follows:

1.	Manufacturing: Cement, steel, plastics	31%
2.	Electricity	27%
3.	Food Industry: Plants, animals	19%
4.	Transportation: Cars, trains, planes	16%
5.	Heating and refrigeration	7%
	TOTAL	**100%**

The above lists of the main activities that cause GHG emissions, help direct and focus the efforts to address the sources of climate change. This will become clearer in the next sections of this chapter. Different companies, and banks and financial institutions can work on addressing GHG emissions in different ways according to the activities they are involved in, or finance.

The sources of greenhouse gases are numerous, but they are dominated by the use of fossil fuels to generate energy. An estimated 75% of all the 50 gigatons of carbon equivalent generated globally in 2019 was a result of the usage of fossil fuels to generate energy.

The sources of GHGs in the U.S. give a good indication of the sources of GHGs globally. These were as follows in 2019 according to the U.S. Energy Information Administration (EIA):

	Of Total GHG
Petroleum	33.3%
Natural Gas	26.7%
Coal	14.1%
Subtotal	**74.1%**
Methane	10.1%
Nitrous Oxide	7.0%
GWP Gases	2.7%
Other CO2	6.1%
Total	**100.00%**

In the U.S., energy from fossil fuels accounted for 74.1% of all GHGs in 2019.

Fossil fuels are mainly petroleum, natural gas, and coal. The main producers of GHGs, per unit of energy produced, are coal, followed by petroleum, then natural gas. In other words, natural gas is "cleaner" than oil, and oil cleaner than coal. The GHGs emitted by burning natural gas to produce a unit of energy, are half of those produced by burning coal.

It is clear from the above table that energy is the largest source of GHGs. Fossil fuels cause 74% of total carbon dioxide and its equivalent emissions in the U.S., and almost an equal percentage globally. Our discussion on climate change will therefore focus mainly on how the world, individual countries, and organizations and banks would manage energy in order to manage GHG emissions.

We will now turn to the "energy mix" that exists in the world today, and which is responsible for 75% of all GHG emissions. We will then look at how this energy mix is expected to change to achieve Net Zero Emissions (NZE) in 2050. Other efforts to limit or reduce carbon dioxide in the atmosphere will then be discussed, and these will be put in the context of the global Paris Accord to achieve Net Zero. We will finally sum up what banks can do, and what they need to disclosure, about the efforts to achieve carbon neutrality, and then net zero.

ENERGY MIX: CLIMATE CHANGE

Energy "Mix" and Achieving Net Zero:

Energy is absolutely critical for economic growth. In turn economic growth is the main factor behind the demand for energy. However, energy, as we have seen, is the main source of greenhouse gases and climate change.

There are many sources of energy, and not all these sources produce greenhouse gases. The general term used to describe the different sources of energy is "energy mix." It is necessary to give an overview of the energy mix that exists at the timing of the writing of this book in 2021, and how this mix is expected to be in 2050 if net zero emissions (NZE) are to be achieved globally.

Economic growth would come from both an expected increase in population growth, and in the standard of living (per-capita income). Both of these components have historically been highly correlated with an increase in the demand for energy. It is therefore reasonable to assume that there would be a significant increase in the demand and consumption of energy by 2050.

Some forecasts however assume that there would be a "decoupling" of economic growth, and the increase in demand for energy. This would happen mainly because of behavioral changes, and more energy efficiencies.

In all cases it is reasonable to assume that there would be an increase in the demand for energy by 2050. One main issue is how much the increase in energy demand would be. The other issue is how much clean energy would be produced and/or consumed.

We will now define where the world stands now on the energy mix. We will then present the expectations of where this energy mix would be in 2050 if net zero is to be achieved. We will after that list the main steps needed to achieve the 2050 energy mix. These steps are the ones that companies and banks would be expected to follow in general, but each according to its circumstances and capacity.

The International Energy Agency, IEA, issued in May 2021 a landmark report on the relationship between energy and how to achieve net zero. The report is aptly titled "Net Zero by 2050: A roadmap for the Global Energy Sector." This report has become instantly a main reference for how the global energy markets are expected to develop in the next 30 years to achieve net zero by 2050.

Emerging/developing countries are expected to play an important role in these developments. The banks in the emerging markets would be expected to take the lead in initiating and financing many of the investments needed in this sector.

We should note that we will focus on the supply of energy in the energy mix. This is because total energy consumption is generally less than energy supply, because a lot of energy (possibly 25%) is lost in transmission, inefficiencies, etc.

According to the IEA the energy mix in 2020, and the "ideal" energy mix (from the supply side) in 2050 are the following:

	2020	2050
Oil	29%	8%
Natural Gas	23%	11%
Coal	26%	4%
Fossil Fuels	78%	23%
Nuclear	5	11
Renewables	12	67
Solar	1	20
Wind	1	16
Hydroelectric	3	6
Biofuels	6	20
Other Renewables	1	6
Total	100%	100%

This 2050 energy supply mix is provided to illustrate the need to take many steps to achieve it. The actual mix in 2050 is likely to be very different, as any forecast for 30 years, which also includes hundreds of variables is very likely to be. Moreover, some of the IEA's expectations might be viewed as aspirational by some. However, the "direction," and steps the IEA mentions as needed to reach this are generally agreed upon.

The IEA is one of the main global organizations working on the plans to achieve Net Zero Emission (NZE) by 2050. Others include the IPCC (the Intergovernmental Panel on Climate Change). The IEA is possibly among the most aggressive in calling for drastic measures to achieve net zero by 2050.

There are several other organizations that have put out plans to achieve net zero. Shell, the oil company, has published a very well-thought-out report on how to achieve this. The report, which is called "Sky, Meeting the Goals of the Paris Agreement" tries to be realistic – as it factors in business considerations. Another credible overall plan is the one put forward by Bill Gates in his 2021 book "How to Avoid a Climate Disaster."

The U.S. Energy Information Administration, E.I.A., also puts out well-thought-out global energy forecasts/outlook. Although the EIA's focus is on the U.S., its conclusions appear to differ from those of the IEA. Its projections in early 2021 point out that the U.S. crude oil production in 2050 would most likely be at the same levels as those in 2020. The same would apply to natural gas. If we apply the same U.S. trends globally, the expectations are that the production (and consumption) of oil and gas would remain at their same levels in 2020, but coal would decrease. However, renewable energy would significantly increase in the energy mix. The overall consumption of energy would also increase by around 10%.

It is best to go deeper into the "case study" of the U.S. energy sector, because the energy mix in the U.S. mirrors the energy mix globally from both the production (supply) and consumption (demand) points of view. Moreover, the Energy Information Agency (EIA) of the U.S. has excellent statistics, and market-oriented plans that make discussing this case realistic.

The energy sources used by the U.S. in 2019 were as follows according to the E.I.A.:

Petroleum	37%
Natural Gas	32%
Coal	11%
Nuclear Electric	8%
Renewable Energy:	11%
Solar	9%
Wind	24%
Hydroelectric	22%
Biofuels	20%
Biomass Waste	4%
Geothermal	2%
Wood	20%

We will now give a brief discussion of each of these energy sources in the energy mix, and the expectations for the growth (or otherwise) in the supply/demand for each.

Fossil fuels in the U.S. were almost 80% of total energy sources in 2020. Petroleum/oil was the largest source, and almost all of it has been produced in the U.S. itself. The expectation is that oil production in the U.S. would remain at its current levels in 2050. However, its share in the energy mix of the U.S. would decline, because the overall demand for energy is expected to increase in 2050. Natural gas supply is also expected to remain at its current levels, or possibly increase, because NGL is the "cleanest" among fossil fuels.

Coal, on the other hand, is expected to decline significantly in 2050 under almost all scenarios in absolute amounts (and certainly as a percentage of the energy mix).

Nuclear energy has been the main unknown in the energy supply in the U.S., and globally. It is certainly a clean source of energy. However, safety issues have haunted it globally, including accidents in the U.S.

itself, Russia, and Japan. The general expectation is that the supply of nuclear energy would remain the same in 2050. This is notwithstanding that nuclear energy can be a main producer of electricity, and electricity is generally expected to become the main end-use energy globally in 2050.

Renewable energy accounted for only 11% of energy supply in the U.S. in 2020. All forecasts expect major growth in the supply of renewable energy in 2050, both in absolute amounts, and as a share of the larger energy mix. Actually, the only sources of energy that have increased during the Covid global recession are renewables. The production of energy from solar and wind power has increased. This is at a time when both oil and gas production declined.

Solar energy will most likely be the main source of renewable energy in 2050. The growth in the demand for solar energy has been driven by more than aspirations and plans to have clean energy. This demand has been driven mainly by very large and consistent decline in the cost of generating solar energy over the last 20 years. This has made solar energy competitive with other sources of energy.

Solar energy and its growth are dependent on factors other than pure cost. They are dependent also on what we in this book call the four "S"s and two "T"s: Sun, Space, Storage, Stability, Technology and Transmission. Solar needs to be in places with abundant sun most of the year. Moreover, Solar needs space (real estate). Storage solutions of energy produced is needed because of "downtime" at night. And solar needs to be where there is stability of the political system. Technology has been progressing at remarkable levels resulting in lower cost. Finally, solar needs to have transmission methods that are economical. These factors make North and Sub-Sahara Africa, Egypt, the Gulf countries, the U.S., and Australia among the best possible locations for very large solar "manufacturing plants."

Solar is particularly relevant also because it can be used to generate electricity – the form of energy usage that is most likely to witness the largest increase until 2050.

Electricity is a preferred energy medium for many reasons. Not least among these is that the infrastructure that is used to transmit and use electricity can remain the same with the transition from fossil fuels to clean energy. This comes from the fact electricity has three phases: generation, transmission, and usage. Only the generation part would need to change by 2050. Of course the "usage" part needs major infrastructure investments as well. For example, electric vehicles need to have ready access to "sockets" all over their routes, which need to be installed.

A form of energy that does not statistically appear in the energy mix tables of 2020, will likely have a significant share in 2050. This is hydrogen. Several new investments are going into hydrogen production because it can be a clean source of energy, although it is currently expensive to produce. A collection of practitioners focusing on hydrogen production have formed "the Hydrogen Council" to coordinate their efforts, as they obviously expect hydrogen production / consumption to increase significantly. However, hydrogen remains a "slow moving" source of energy because it is very expensive to produce as we have noted. Nevertheless, going forward, financing of hydrogen generation will be "counted" as an important ESG activity of a bank.

It is now worth mentioning the other sources of renewable energy, although none of these is likely to see the significant growth that solar and hydrogen would see.

Wood is a renewable energy, but it does create carbon dioxide when burnt. Some claim wood is "carbon-neutral" because the burnt wood is replaced by new trees. The evidence is not conclusive on this.

Biofuels are fuels made of biomass. Biofuels also emit carbon dioxide when used for energy production. However, they also take fossil fuel energy to produce them. They nevertheless emit far fewer carbon dioxide than fossil fuel.

Biomass Waste: These are primarily made of waste (both solid and otherwise). Burning biomass releases the same amount of carbon dioxide that these plants capture while growing through photosynthesis. This makes them a carbon-neutral energy source, according to the E.I.A.

Energy demand is expected to increase significantly by 2050, as we have mentioned. This is at a time when the Paris Agreement calls for zero-net carbon-emission in that year. This obviously means that significant increase of non-fossil fuels would need to be produced. The current "energy-mix" would also need to radically change by 2050 if NZE is to be achieved. Nevertheless, the cost of production will remain a determinant factor of what energy is produced / consumed.

Many energy companies are moving to change their energy mix. Energy companies, and energy investors now increasingly have ESG considerations in their long-term investments. "Responsible Investor" now generally means ESG-compliant investor. Some now define carbon footprint in investments.

There are many examples of efforts to substitute fossil energy by no-carbon energy. These include a 2000 mega wat solar power plant in Abu Dhabi, and a 400 mega wat wind power plant in Saudi Arabia. These examples are worth noting because they are in oil producing countries.

Oil companies are moving from being oil investors, to becoming energy investors. BP is a major example of this. Another example is Masdar, which is now a global leader in alternative energy investments. This is noteworthy because Masdar is a UAE company, and the UAE is a major oil exporting country. Masdar is a subsidiary of Mubadala, the UAE's main investment company.

There are de-carbonization efforts in many industries to make them more sustainable. For example AGA, a major aluminum producer, is going to be produced fully "green." Banks can share in these decarbonization efforts by financing them.

Moving from companies to countries, the need of diversification of oil-producing economies away from oil dependency is becoming more urgent. This conforms completely with the movement to achieve net zero in 2050.

Even without an increase in the demand for energy, achieving net-zero by 2050 would require major changes of the global energy mix. The main changes needed would be, first to decrease, or at least stabilize, the growth of the consumption of fossil fuels (this is what the U.S. aims to do). This would come from increased efficiencies, and behavioral changes. The second needed action would be to produce (and consume) more "clean energy." These would be mainly solar, wind, and a "rediscovered" energy source, hydrogen. Third, electrification would increase across all fields. The fourth pillar of the new structure needed to achieve net zero in 2050 would be the removal of carbon dioxide from the atmosphere. This is referred to as CCUS: Carbon capture usage and storage. CCUS is expected to have a major role to achieve NZE by 2050, and we will discuss it in more detail in the next section.

All those involved in the energy-planning process expect a far more diverse energy mix in 2050 than is the case today. They also generally agree on the key steps that need to be taken to achieve net zero and which would include:

1. Behavior and avoided demand
2. Energy Efficiency
3. Hydrogen usage
4. Electrification increases
5. Bioenergy usage
6. Wind increase
7. Solar (major) increases
8. Other fuel shifts
9. CCUS: Carbon capture usage and storage
10. Government policies (incentives, carbon taxes, carbon caps/ trade ...)

There are diverse views of how the Energy Mix in 2050 will look like. It is safe to say however, that for net-zero to be achieved, the points listed above would have to be implemented. Banks would need to take similar steps, or encourage their stakeholders to take these steps, and/or finance these measures.

CARBON CAPTURE, UTILIZATION, AND STORAGE: CCUS

One solution that can potentially be very significant to achieve net-zero carbon emissions, is to reduce the presence of existing carbon dioxide in the atmosphere. This involves carbon capture, then utilizing this carbon, or storing it. These processes are called carbon capture utilization and storage (CCUS). CCUS can be effective to neutralize the impact of the continued usage of fossil fuels.

CCUS is broken down into two parts: CCU, and CCS. Carbon Capture and Utilization (CCU) involves the conversion (or utilization) of captured carbon dioxide into other materials that take out carbon dioxide as a greenhouse gas. On the other hand, Carbon Capture and Storage (CCS) involves the storage of captured carbon dioxide underground. Carbon would be stored out of the atmosphere, hence would not have a role in global warming.

Carbon capture can be through two ways. The first is Direct Air Capture (DAC), where a factory can be put anywhere and "suck out" carbon from the air. This is an expensive process, partly because carbon exists in small particles in the air. Moreover, GHGs other than carbon dioxide are not captured in these processes.

The more effective way is to capture carbon at the major sources where it is emitted, or "Point Capture." This would involve putting devices to remove the carbon dioxide mainly emitted in cement plants, steel plants, plastics plants, and oil extraction sites and refineries (where gas is flared).

The cost of CCUS is still very expensive, ranging from $200 to 100 per ton of carbon dioxide.

CCUS devices can become more in use if incentives are increased to have them, or if the cost of not having them is increased. Both measures would involve government interventions, and policies. As governments start imposing a "price" on carbon emissions, possibly through taxes, CCUS projects would become more economically feasible. Essentially governments would try to make emissions more expensive, and removing them (including by negative emissions) less expensive. A third, and potentially the best way to make CCUS more feasible would be to have technological innovations that would reduce the cost of CCUS.

All credible forecasts of the measures needed to achieve NZE by 2050 now include a major role for CCUS. The parties expecting major usage of CCUS range from the IEA, to the EIA to the major oil companies.

It is estimated that 90% of carbon dioxide emissions from large emission players (like cement factories) can be captured. The fact however is that the cost of CCUS processes appear still high. This makes the viability of CCUS projects not certain. Nevertheless, CCUS activities have started in earnest. The I.E.A. reports that there are currently 18 major CCUS projects worldwide in 2021.

The most environmentally-friendly carbon-removal and sequestration efforts are the "natural" ones involving agriculture. There are a variety of these natural activities that help capture carbon, and store it. These natural processes fall under two broad categories for the general reader: a) increased forestation, and farming, and b) better use of soil.

Increased forestation captures carbon dioxide naturally. The process should ensure however that captured carbon is not sent back into the atmosphere, through burning of wood or similar processes. Keeping carbon of trees out of the atmosphere involves, for example, the increased usage of wood in everyday life, such as in buildings.

CCUS can be a game changer for climate change if there are technological innovations that make the processes of utilization and/or storage more financially viable. Bill Gates has cited CCUS as one of the major areas that can be effective in achieving net zero by 2050. This came in his 2021 book "How to Avoid a Climate Disaster." He also mentions that CCUS is one of the areas that can become much more economically scalable if it gets enough Research and Development funding.

CCUS is likely to be one of the main methods that will be focused on to achieve net-zero. This is because CCUS helps neutralize the carbon emissions of fossil fuels, and because fossil fuels are reasonably expected to continue to be a main part of the "energy mix" until 2050. Moreover, major investments have been going into the fossil petroleum and natural gas industries, and their returns would usually take a long time to be realized. Fossil fuels are also expected to continue to have low-cost of production. Some argues that it is economically effective to continue to use fossil fuels to some extent – which would be much more acceptable from the environmental point of view if the carbon dioxide emissions from them is neutralized.

Because CCUS activities are likely to be a major focus of efforts to achieve net zero, they should be measured and monitored to the extent possible. Companies and banks can do that by reporting the carbon dioxide captured, and removed through utilization or storage. The reports can include the CCUS activities of the bank itself, or those activities that are financed by the bank. Governments can encourage CCUS activities through different incentives that would make them more financially viable, at least in their earlier stages.

The metrics that can be used to measure CCUS can be:

- Carbon dioxide captured and utilized and stored by the company or bank,
- Financing of companies that are involved in CCS, or CCU.
- Support to permanent forestation and agriculture.
- Support and involvement in carbon markets.

In order to increase the development and wide usage of CCUS factories and devices, carbon markets need to be further developed to allow for trade of the carbon dioxide captured through CCUS processes. One way to do that is to have a more aggressive usage of CCUS in offset calculations. We will discuss the role of carbon markets in the next section.

CARBON MARKETS

Carbon markets, like any market, involve demand and supply. The unit traded is called a "carbon credit," and is equivalent to one metric ton of carbon dioxide (or its GHG equivalent). Carbon markets can serve to intermediate between those who have GHG emissions (and therefore demand carbon credits), and those who supply carbon credits. The suppliers of carbon credits have activities that a) avoid, b) reduce, and/or c) capture and remove carbon through usage or storage (CCUS). This transaction is generally called carbon-offset.

The buyers of carbon credits are those who need to reduce their carbon emissions either involuntarily or voluntarily.

Governments have started to impose "caps" on carbon emissions for many companies. This imposes involuntary carbon reduction goals that companies have to meet, if their emissions are more than the assigned "caps." The way to reduce carbon emissions and stay within a cap is to purchase carbon credits. Canada has a good well defined "cap and trade program." The largest global mandatory "cap and trade" programs are the European Emissions Trading Schemes (EU-ETS). Countries have started also to levy carbon taxes, which can be reduced by acquiring carbon offsets.

Voluntary reductions come about from countries and companies who have committed to reach net-zero by a certain date. Countries have commitments to reduce their national emissions under their Nationally Determined Contributions (NDC) plans, as per the Paris Agreement (which we will discuss in the next section).

Hundreds of companies and banks worldwide have also committed to have net-zero by certain dates. These include the likes of Google, Microsoft, Walmart, BP, Total, J.P. Morgan, Citibank, BlackRock, etc. These companies and banks would need to buy carbon credits if they cannot meet their self-proclaimed emission-reduction targets on their own.

The suppliers of carbon credits are those who have activities that avoid, reduce and/or capture and use or store carbon (CCUS as mentioned earlier).

Those who avoid carbon emissions altogether are mainly the producers of clean energy. Solar, wind, nuclear, and geothermal projects create carbon credits when they produce energy that does not produce GHGs.

Avoidance of GHGs comes also from reforestation, as we have seen in the section on GHGs.

The entities that reduce emissions by increasing the efficiency of their fossil-fuel operations create carbon credits equal to the reduced emissions (compared to emissions before efficiency measures were introduced.

Carbon Capture Usage and Storage (CCUS) is the most straight forward supplier of carbon credits. Carbon credits from CCUS are equal to how much GHG emissions are removed from the atmosphere (directly or at source, as we have shown in the CCUS section of this chapter).

In addition to having suppliers/sellers, and buyers of carbon credits, there are some important "process management" requirements for carbon markets to function. The first is that independent certification should exist that verifies the authenticity and accuracy of the carbon credit (mostly at the supplier side). The certificate can be produced according to one of the standards that have recently been developed (and keep developing). Second, there needs to be a carbon-exchange where buy/sell transactions are made and registered.

There would also be a need eventually to have regulation of these markets. There would moreover be the need for assurance from independent third parties to verify the whole process (especially in the books of the buyers and sellers of carbon credits).

Carbon markets (and transactions) can be within a country, or across countries. Many believe that developed countries can be net buyers of carbon credits from emerging countries. The banks in the emerging countries can play a significant role in facilitating and intermediating these transactions.

Banks can finance carbon-credit-creating-projects. They can also play a role in intermediating carbon credits buy/sell transactions, whether these transactions are inter-country, or intra-country.

Banks can report on how many carbon credits they helped create through financing of carbon credit creating projects. They can also report on any intermediating activity they have in the carbon markets.

THE PARIS AGREEMENT ON CLIMATE CHANGE

Our discussion of climate change, greenhouse emissions, and the energy mix needed to reach net zero by 2050 all fit under the global framework to reach net zero, generally referred to as the Paris Accord. It is necessary to go over the broad outline of this agreement because it has implications of what banks are expected to do in this area over the next thirty years.

The Paris Accord, or Agreement, is the much acclaimed international agreement signed in Paris on December 12, 2015 at COP21. It came into effect on November 4, 2016. COP21 is one of the periodic UN climate change conferences, the latest of which is COP26 on November 9-19, 2021 in Glasgow Scotland. COP stands for "Conference of the Parties."

The Paris agreement's main goal is to limit global warming to 1.5 degrees Celsius compared to pre-industrial levels, but in all cases below 2 degrees. The aim is to achieve global net zero by 2050. This would be mainly by limiting greenhouse gas emissions.

According to the IPCC, the world has already reached 1 degree Celsius in 2017 above that of pre-industrial times (defined as 1850-1900). This is the reference period when global climate data is available.

The global reference temperature is defined as the combined temperature over land, and above sea. It should be noted that several countries have already witnessed average temperatures of more than 1.5°C over the reference period.

The human-induced global warming of +1.5 degrees will be reached by 2040 if unchecked. The most realistic expectations are that global temperatures will exceed +1.5 degrees before 2050, but would go down to 1.5 degrees if necessary actions are taken. This is the scenario the IPCC calls "overshoot pathway."

Each country is expected to submit a national plan to achieve this target globally. These plans are called nationally determined contributions – NDCs. Most countries have submitted their first NDCs, and have updated them for COP26 in November 2021.

The NDCs are expected to cover two main elements a) the national action plans to reduce GHGs to reach global goals, and b) actions to build resilience to adapt to the impacts of rising temperatures. The second part is necessary because global temperatures are expected to continue to increase until net zero carbon emissions is achieved.

Disclosure under the Paris Agreement is expected to be a formal process under what is called the Enhanced Transparency Framework (ETF). This would involve country reports starting in 2024. Countries would report a) actions taken, and b) progress in climate change mitigation, adaptation measures, and support provided. The ETF reports would be consolidated under a "Global Stocktake" which will assess global progress towards achieving the goals of the Paris Agreement.

An overshoot pathway would point to a) the need to use CCUS on a scale that current technologies do not appear to support, and b) the need to reduce sources of GHG emissions aggressively to reach the 2050 Paris goal. There is also the risk, according to the IPCC of irreversible climate induced changes if an overshoot occurs – such as rising sea levels and melting down of ice caps (especially over Antarctica, and Greenland).

It is worth noting that the combined effects of NDCs show that an overshoot is likely to occur because the national action plans do not appear aggressive enough to reach desired targets.

ESG AND THE PARIS ACCORD

There are a number of observations worth noting on the current status of the Paris Agreement as it relates to ESG, and especially in the emerging countries.

The transition phase is likely to be a harsh one for many emerging countries. The Paris Accord notes the need for developed countries to help emerging countries deal with these adverse changes. The Paris Accord, as reconfirmed by COP26 in November 2021, calls for developed countries to assist emerging countries in 3 ways:

1. Financial Assistance: This would help in the mitigation efforts to contain the adverse effects of climate change in these countries.

2. Technology: This calls for technological improvements to a) reduce GHG emissions, and b) improve resilience to climate change.

3. Capacity Building: This would involve developed countries providing assistance to emerging countries to build their capacity to manage climate action.

There are some points worth noting on the assistance to be made in this area:

a. There is a need for developed countries to ensure that they are implementing what they have undertaken to do in the Paris Agreement.

b. There is a need to quantify what this assistance needs to be.

c. The methodology of what the parties would do needs to be better clarified.

d. There does not appear to be effective verification mechanisms of what countries submit in their NDCs (this applies to all countries, and not only emerging ones).

e. Developed countries need to verify that the assistance they are providing is indeed targeted at climate-related issues, and ESG issues. This verification is necessary because emerging countries have many pressing needs, and they might allocate climate-related assistance to where it is not intended.

Banks in the emerging countries can play a crucial role in helping to achieve climate-related goals. This is mainly because of the relatively major roles banks play in their emerging countries. Banks in the emerging countries can play a major role in channeling the needed assistance from the developed countries. It would be more effective for emerging-market banks to do that, given that their human resources and technology capabilities are usually the better ones in their countries. The verification process we mentioned in the earlier point would also be easier if assistance is channeled through these banks.

MEASURES NEEDED TO ACHIEVE NET ZERO IN 2050

It is generally accepted that the world will significantly increase its carbon and GHG emissions if economic growth continues to be fueled by the current mix of energy sources. Net-zero emissions by 2050 will not be achieved if this trend is not changed, and if economic growth is to continue. There is a general agreement that the following measures would need to be taken to achieve both a) economic growth, and b) net-zero emissions by 2050. These measures are selected from different programs, and banks in the emerging countries would be expected to follow their implementation:

1. Fossil fuels will continue to be used, and demanded. However, efforts would be made to limit their use to the extent possible.
2. There will be more focus on using the more carbon-efficient of the fossil fuels. These are a) natural gas, then b) petroleum, then c) coal, in that order. Coal would be phased out.
3. Efforts will continue to improve energy efficiencies where fossil fuels need to be used. An example of better fossil fuel efficiency is the improvement of fuel efficiency of aeroplanes.
4. Carbon capture utilization and storage (CCUS) would have to increase very significantly. This would allow for the partial reduction of carbon present in the atmosphere because of emissions from fossil fuels.
5. "Carbon offset" programs will be more widely used. These programs would involve the offsetting of carbon emissions by those who have carbon emission activities. They would do that by purchasing "carbon credits," or carbon offsets that would result in their achieving net zero, or net reduction of their emissions.
6. Renewable and clean energy: Production will increase exponentially. "Clean" energy sources will continue to increase their share in the energy "mix." Renewable energy sources would come mostly from solar power. Other sources would be wind, hydrogen, geothermal, and nuclear energy.

7. Increased efficiencies in electric power generation would increase. This would include the increase in battery-powered engines, and battery storage capacities.
8. Technological improvements will continue to be needed to achieve net zero. Research and development efforts would be increasingly important. More digitization is also needed as it can be "environmentally-friendly." This includes the example of working from home.
9. Financing of all the above measures to achieve net zero would be needed.

Banks, whatever their size, need to plan these nine activities, implement and/or finance them, and disclose/report them.

The "balanced" measures that a bank, or company needs to have regarding climate change are the following:

1. Calculation of Own Carbon Footprint: This is the equivalent of all greenhouse gases emitted in Scopes 1, 2 by the bank itself. This is measured by metric tons carbon dioxide equivalent as described earlier in this chapter.
2. Calculation of Carbon Footprint from financial activities. This involves the calculation of the GHG emitted by activities financed by the bank. This is the equivalent of Scope 3 emissions. Banks do not need to do this in the first years of reporting, but should start calculating data.
3. Financing of activities to achieve net zero. These are mainly the first eight activities mentioned above. Financing these measures is the most important role of a bank, especially in the emerging markets.
4. Participation in carbon markets.

It should be noted that "carbon neutral certification" of certain projects, which are available in many countries, generally cover the above four points. The process usually also involves having progress reports.

2

ENVIRONMENTAL GOALS: THE ECOSYSTEM

INTRODUCTION

WE HAVE ADDRESSED IN THE previous chapter the environmental concerns related to climate change, and what role banks and companies can play to tackle them. In this chapter we will discuss the main environmental concerns that are not directly climate-related. These are environmental issues that go beyond climate change and are of major concern to all countries. Some of these issues are of particular concern to emerging economies. They include water scarcity and cleanliness, air pollution, pollution in the seas, and mounting waste management problems among others.

These issues have been very well defined in a United Kingdom commissioned report under a team headed by Professor Partha Dasgupta of Cambridge University. This report, which was issued in February 2021 and is now known as the Dasgupta report, has quickly come to be generally regarded as a roadmap of what needs to be done to preserve the ecosystem. The report complements several other efforts being carried out by other private and public sector organizations, including their work on ESG.

It is worthwhile giving the Dasgupta report's "overview" of what needs to be done before we go into specific areas of concern, and what banks and companies can do in this space.

The Dasgupta report says that the demands created by the increase in human population and prosperity, far exceed nature's capacity to supply humanity with the goods and services we all rely on. As a result, "Biodiversity is declining faster than at any time in human history." This is an environmental factor, but different from climate change.

The ecosystems we have are being degraded at unprecedented rates. For emerging economies, or "low income countries" as the Dasgupta report calls them, "these economies are more reliant than high income countries on nature's goods and services from within their borders, and stand to lose the most." This points out the need for those emerging countries to act to sustain the ecosystem, and their banks can play a major role in these endeavors. Developed economies can also help emerging economies deal with the problems of the ecosystem.

As with climate change "reversing these trends requires action now." Action on the ecosystem would in turn help address climate change and Social goals in the Dasgupta report. The report says that action to "coax the ecosystem back to health would help us achieve wider Social goals, and addressing climate change and eliminating poverty."

Food production is the most significant driver of terrestrial biodiversity loss, according to the Dasgupta report. As the global population grows, the enormous problem of producing sufficient food in a sustainable manner will only intensify.

The Dasgupta report, like others, puts a lot of faith in the potential of technological innovations to solve the problems of the ecosystem. This is similar to the expectations that technological innovations can help address climate change (for example CCUS), as discussed in the previous chapter.

Technological innovations and sustainable food production systems "can decrease the sector's contribution to climate change, land-use change and ocean degradation; reduce environmentally damaging inputs and waste; improve production system resilience, through methods such as precision agriculture, integrated pest management and molecular breeding techniques; and are likely to have a positive economic impact, including the creation of jobs."

The Dasgupta report does link climate change to biodiversity loss. The report says, correctly, that decarbonising our energy systems is a necessary part of balancing demand and supply in the ecosystem.

Banks, and the financial system can play a major role in helping to address the increasing threats to the ecosystem. The U.K. report comes to the conclusion that there is a need for "a financial system that channels financial investments – public and private – towards economic activities that enhance our stock of natural assets and encourage sustainable consumption and production activities."

Financial regulators are also expected to mandate assessment of "the systemic extent of nature-related financial risks." Regulators would help encourage the development of "a set of global standards underpinned by credible, decision-grade data, which businesses and financial institutions can use to fully integrate Nature-related considerations into their decision-making, and assess and disclose their use of, and impact on, Nature."

The role of banks and financial institutions is broadly defined by the Dasgupta report as one of "accounting for dependencies and impacts on Nature in their activities; and through the measurement and disclosure, not only of climate-related financial risks but Nature-related financial risks too."

We will now discuss the many areas in the environmental part of ESG where banks and companies need to have an important role to address issues that go beyond climate change.

We have addressed in the previous chapter the environmental concerns related to climate change, and what role banks and companies can play to tackle them. In this chapter we will discuss the main environmental concerns that are not directly climate-related. These are environmental issues that go beyond climate change and are of major concern to all countries. Some of these issues are of particular concern to emerging economies. They include water scarcity and cleanliness, air pollution, pollution in the seas, and mounting waste management problems among others.

These issues have been very well defined in a United Kingdom commissioned report under a team headed by Professor Partha Dasgupta of Cambridge University. This report, which was issued in February 2021 and is now known as the Dasgupta report, has quickly come to be generally regarded as a roadmap of what needs to be done to preserve the ecosystem. The report complements several other efforts being carried out by other private and public sector organizations, including their work on ESG.

It is worthwhile giving the Dasgupta report's "overview" of what needs to be done before we go into specific areas of concern, and what banks and companies can do in this space.

The Dasgupta report says that the demands created by the increase in human population and prosperity, far exceed nature's capacity to supply humanity with the goods and services we all rely on. As a result, "Biodiversity is declining faster than at any time in human history." This is an environmental factor, but different from climate change.

The ecosystems we have are being degraded at unprecedented rates. For emerging economies, or "low income countries" as the Dasgupta report calls them, "these economies are more reliant than high income countries on nature's goods and services from within their borders, and stand to lose the most." This points out the need for those emerging countries to act to sustain the ecosystem, and their banks can play a major role in these endeavours. Developed economies can also help emerging economies deal with the problems of the ecosystem.

As with climate change "reversing these trends requires action now." Action on the ecosystem would in turn help address climate change and Social goals in the Dasgupta report. The report says that action to "coax the ecosystem back to health would help us achieve wider Social goals, and addressing climate change and eliminating poverty."

Food production is the most significant driver of terrestrial biodiversity loss, according to the Dasgupta report. As the global population grows, the enormous problem of producing sufficient food in a sustainable manner will only intensify.

The Dasgupta report, like others, puts a lot of faith in the potential of technological innovations to solve the problems of the ecosystem. This is similar to the expectations that technological innovations can help address climate change (for example CCUS), as discussed in the previous chapter.

Technological innovations and sustainable food production systems "can decrease the sector's contribution to climate change, land-use change and ocean degradation; reduce environmentally damaging inputs and waste; improve production system resilience, through methods such as precision agriculture, integrated pest management and molecular breeding techniques; and are likely to have a positive economic impact, including the creation of jobs."

The Dasgupta report does link climate change to biodiversity loss. The report says, correctly, that decarbonising our energy systems is a necessary part of balancing demand and supply in the ecosystem.

Banks, and the financial system can play a major role in helping to address the increasing threats to the ecosystem. The U.K. report comes to the conclusion that there is a need for "a financial system that channels financial investments – public and private – towards economic activities that enhance our stock of natural assets and encourage sustainable consumption and production activities."

Financial regulators are also expected to mandate assessment of "the systemic extent of nature-related financial risks." Regulators would help encourage the development of "a set of global standards underpinned by credible, decision-grade data, which businesses and financial institutions can use to fully integrate Nature-related considerations into their decision-making, and assess and disclose their use of, and impact on, Nature."

The role of banks and financial institutions is broadly defined by the Dasgupta report as one of "accounting for dependencies and impacts on Nature in their activities; and through the measurement and disclosure, not only of climate-related financial risks but Nature-related financial risks too."

We will now discuss the many areas in the environmental part of ESG where banks and companies need to have an important role to address issues that go beyond climate change.

WATER SCARCITY AND SANITATION

Water availability, and water cleanliness are major ESG issues to be addresses globally, especially in the emerging markets. These water issues fit very well into the overall ESG framework, because they meet the two main "eligibility criteria" we have mentioned earlier. These are that there is a major need for action on water issues, and the impact of investments and action can be very significant in addressing these needs. We will discuss in this section what the main issues are concerning water, and how banks, and companies, can address them.

The UN reports that "Worldwide, one in three people do not have access to safe drinking water, and two out of five people do not have a basic hand-washing facility ..."

Moreover, according to the World Resources Institute (WRI), almost 3.5 billion people could face water scarcity by 2025. This is because water demand is projected to rise continuously with economic and population growth, while the increase in water supply will be limited. Natural water supplies are actually going down because of the effects of climate change.

Water stress is also increasing – where water stress is defined by the UN as "the withdrawal of too much fresh water from natural sources compared with fresh water available." Around 2 billion people are now estimated to live in countries with high levels of water stress.

The EU defines water scarcity as the imbalance between water availability, and water demand exceeding supply from natural resources.

Drought also affects water supply (on a temporary basis), because of a decrease in rainfall. Climate change has been increasingly causing water draught, and a decrease in the supply of fresh water.

Water supply can moreover be impacted by the quality of water. Water pollution can affect the supply of fresh, drinkable water.

The European Union's management (and measurement) of water scarcity appears to be the most developed worldwide. This is remarkable because Europe has also the least pressing water problems from a scarcity point of view, and virtually none from a sanitation/cleanliness point of view.

The most common way to measure water scarcity is the Water Exploitation Index (WEI). The WEI is the average demand for freshwater (in a country or region), divided by the long-term average water resources.

The UN SDG's (Sustainable Development Goals) has goal number 6 dealing with water. It calls to "Ensure availability and sustainable management of water, and sanitation for all." Goal 6 essentially has two sub-goals: a) safely managed drinking water, and b) safely managed sanitation.

It is a basic fact that water scarcity, and water sanitation are now major problems globally. These water problems are also challenges found most acutely in emerging countries. Some developed countries do have water scarcity issues, but none have water cleanliness issues worth mentioning. Water is mostly an emerging countries problem, and an existential one at that in some countries.

It is therefore unsurprising that many emerging countries make water management a main goal of theirs. Investments in increasing water availability and sanitation would also have the largest impact in emerging countries. The task is to make investments in water rewarding from the financial point of view. The impact will be felt in the "environmental" part of ESG, but would certainly affect the "social" part as well.

WHAT BANKS AND COMPANIES CAN DO ABOUT WATER

Addressing water availability and cleanliness is necessary especially in high-water-stress countries, and banks and companies need to report on these two elements. The World Resources Institute (WRI) gives a rating of water stress levels for most countries of the world. There are five WRI water stress categories: Extremely High, High, Medium-High, Low-Medium, and Low. Banks and companies in countries in the first 3 categories should report on their consumption of water, when they start reporting on ESG. In later years, they can measure and report on water consumption of their clients as well.

The second important measure of water is water cleanliness. In this case, any initiative that a bank or company might have to increase water cleanliness can be reported. This relates to the second part of SDG number 6.

Banks can also report on any water initiative they have, or support. These initiatives would be to reduce water consumption and withdrawal, or increase the supply of fresh water. These initiatives can be profitable if water is priced correctly. This is mostly up to governments to determine.

A bank should give a lot of "weight" of the impact to the measures of water availability in any plans it has. This is especially in countries with high water-stress levels.

The need to give attention to water scarcity and sanitation is a major reason why a balanced approach is needed in ESG – where several factors need to be focused on, in addition to those related to climate change. This is notwithstanding that one can make the argument that the main global environmental problem is climate change, because it affects several other factors, including water scarcity. Climate change is now believed to be one of the main causes of increasing water scarcity, for climate change causes droughts, and increasing desertification in many countries.

The third water metric relates to SDG 14, "Life Below Water." SDG goal 14 aims to "conserve and sustainably use the oceans, seas and marine resources for sustainable development." We will discuss this in the following separate section.

The main water metric is well covered by the Sustainability Accounting Standards Board. However a bank or company does not need to go into detail on water management. A bank's reporting details should depend on its relative size, as per the proportionality principles.

Financial institutions and banks have developed specific instruments to address water issues. These include Blue bonds and Desalination bonds, which are new innovations in finance. The proceeds from these bonds are mainly aimed at reaching SDG goal number 14 (Life below water).

Nordic Investment Bank issued in early 2019 an SEK 2 billion (around $220 million) five year blue bond. Its proceed would finance projects that include "wastewater treatment, prevention of water pollution, and water related climate change adaptation."

Morgan Stanley issued $10 million blue bonds aimed at cleaning plastic pollution in oceans, which is one of the subjects we will discuss in a separate section of this chapter.

WATER DESALINATION

Water desalination is increasingly gaining ground as an important tool to solve the drinkable water scarcity problems.

The need/demand for drinkable water has been driving investments in desalination plants around the world. These investments are also being driven by two economic factors on the supply side a) the reduction in the cost of desalinating water on one hand, and b) the increase in the cost of naturally available water on the other.

There is currently an estimated 20,000 desalination plants globally, which produce drinkable water to around 300 million people. Saudi Arabia is the largest producer of desalinated water, accounting for close to 20% of all desalinated water produced globally.

Desalination processes are all energy-intensive. They are, generally, either a) thermal, or b) electrical/mechanical using reverse-osmosis. The thermal processes use energy to heat sea water that is vaporized then distilled and collected as clean fresh water. The mechanical processes usually use pressure to force sea water into membranes that leave salt trapped on one side, and clean water out on the other side.

The energy-water balance would be most effective if the source of energy used for desalination is renewable, such as solar or wind. These are the best of environmental solutions: both reducing GHGs, and increasing fresh water. Two of the largest such plants that have "two positives" from an environmental point of view (using solar energy to desalinate sea water) are now located in the UAE and in Saudi Arabia.

Desalination energy efficiencies can be the result of factors other than the usage of renewable sources. These would include locating desalination plants with power plants, and/or using energy to produce electricity in the desalination processes.

The production of clean water from desalination is set to increase in the coming years. Improvement in desalination technology is likely to continue and make the production of fresh water more affordable. But even without that, production of fresh water will increase.

The negative impacts from desalination on marine life can be significant if not properly managed. These include a) the brine water left out of the processes, and b) the intake machines that suck and kill small fish and other marine life with the sea water they suck to desalinate.

The size of desalination plants varies. Some might be relatively small, in which case they can be useful for small communities.

Desalination plants, in one form or another, now exist in 183 countries. The water produced by desalination is estimated at around 89 million cubic meters a day, according to the International Desalination Association.

Abu Dhabi is teaming up with the Spanish company Abengoa to build the world's largest solar powered desalination plant. It would use the reverse-osmosis processes. Solar powered plants are estimated to generate a cubic-meter of clean water with a fraction of the energy needed by thermal (3 kWh/m^3 vs 17 kWh/ m^3).

The Dubai Electricity and Water Authority (Dewa) has plans to produce 100% of desalinated water by a mix of clean energy and "waste" heat. Dewa plans to increase its clean water capacity in Dubai to 750 MIGD (million imperial gallons per day) from 470 MIGD. The current process co-generates electricity and water. This would be mainly through a project to be commissioned in 2024.

BANKS AND WATER DESALINATION

A balanced approach to ESG needs to take into account both the carbon emissions from water desalination processes, and the benefits of having water available to communities in need of water.

Clean water availability is a high priority goal for all communities, rich and poor. The need for water in some cases outbalances the possible need to use fossil fuel in its production.

A bank may use financing of desalination plants, large or small, as a positive contribution to ESG.

We believe that ideally, there should be an "offset program" to allow the generation of clean water to offset the emission of carbon dioxide. This is because the lack of fresh water is as serious an issue for many communities as climate change is. A holistic approach to ESG would take all ESG factors into consideration.

Some companies link the two goals together. The MAF Group in the UAE has made it a goal to be net positive in both carbon and water by 2040. They aim to produce more clean water in 2040 than they use. The Group was awarded the "Green Globe" certification for its Middle East hotel operations.

PLASTICS AND THE SEAS

"Plastic" is one of the main issues that need to be addressed within the overall Environmental part of the ESG framework. There can also be a significant impact from investments and action to address these issues. We will discuss in this section a) the environmental problems related to plastics, and b) how these problems can be resolved, and c) the role of banks and companies can play in this area.

The environmental problems with plastics

Most of the processes that currently produce plastics are a result of energy-intensive, and environmentally unfriendly, processes. Plastics are also made from oil, with 8% of petroleum production going into plastic manufacturing. Plastic production is also expected to almost quadruple by 2050.

However, the main impact of plastics on the environment is the plastic waste that remains in the environment, especially in the seas and oceans. Plastics, especially single-use plastics, are disposable, but not bio-degradable. They also degenerate into very small pieces. It is these "micro plastics" that find their way into animal and human bodies, and cause health problems.

A study by Pew Charitable Trusts found out that there will be two times more plastic each year in the oceans for the next 10 years.

China is reportedly the largest producer of plastic waste, at 60 million tons/year. It is followed by the U.S. which produces 38 million tons/year. These deteriorate into micro-plastics (in soil, water, and food).

A large part of the plastic waste is dumped into the seas and oceans. A 2019 study by the Canadian Parliamentary Research Service found out that "between 4.8 million and 12.7 million tons of plastics enter the world's oceans annually." A 2017 study in "Science Advances" estimates that of all plastics produced globally by 2015, just 9% has been recycled.

One particular plastics problem is the lost and abandoned fishing gear from large-scale fishing. This is now estimated to make up at least 10% of all plastics in the oceans. The so called "ghost gear" is regarded as the most harmful to marine life. This is partly from the fact the gear is mostly made of plastics. However, the more harmful part appears to be the large size of the gear, and its structure. Solving the "ghost gear" problem would best be through international regulations and cooperation. The private sector can realistically do little about regulating the mass fishing, although advocacy can drive governments to act. The private sector and banks can best work to deal with the negative consequences of plastics. This is also generally the issue with all plastics found at sea.

Solving the plastics problem

There is a general agreement that there are several measures that need to be taken to solve the plastics problem. These include:

1. Curbing demand for plastics. Curbing demand for plastics would reduce the amount of plastics being produced.
    Some have called for banning single-use plastics altogether. The banning of single-use plastics necessitates the usage, and production, of alternatives. However, most of the alternatives require manufacturing processes that are energy intensive, which would be more harmful to the environment than plastics.

    Moreover, many of the simple plastic products are very cheap, and are necessities to low-income (and lowest income) groups. This would include low-income countries.

    Some alternatives have also been found to be more unhealthy than single use plastics. For example, multi-use cloth bags are suspected of retaining virus/bacteria, while single use plastics have less risk because they are disposed of. The disposable plastic-gloves are also less risky than any alternatives. Reducing demand for plastics can include:

    a. Putting limits on the use of single-use plastics.
    b. Eliminating unnecessary packaging,
    c. Transitioning to return-and-reuse systems, and
    d. Substituting virgin with recycled plastic or switching to other materials like paper.

2. Better management of plastic waste: The second way to deal with the plastic problem is to better manage plastic waste. This includes:
    a. Capturing plastic waste effectively. This includes plastics on land and sea.
    b. Disposing of plastic waste.

c. Recycling of plastic waste.

Recycling of plastics is an obvious solution to the collected/captured plastic waste. This can be mechanical recycling, or chemical recycling. Mechanical recycling needs to have the plastics sorted out in the first place, and they need to be "clean plastics." Many governments have started to mandate minimum level of recycled contents. The European Union, and California, already have regulations in this regard. Many companies have committed to use chemical processes to recycle plastics.

The chemical recycling solutions are promising. However, most of the chemical recycling processes appear to be energy intensive, because they involve machine-crushing, and high temperatures. This makes the chemical recycling processes not environmentally friendly, and expensive.

Some chemical-recycling start-ups worth noting include Ioniqa Technologies in the Netherlands (involved in Coca Cola production). They also include Carbios (bio-recycling) in France, where the users would include Nestle, Pepsi, and L'Occitane.

The mechanical recycling appears to be the more practical solution for the near future. According to Pew, "mechanical recycling could help prevent up to a third of the plastics produced from polluting the environment." This would include the scaling up of mechanical recycling of bottles and containers - especially those made from PET or the HDPE plastic

Many believe that plastic de-pollution is doable, and many in the private sector have ambitious plans to recycle plastics. For example, Loop Industries agreed with several large companies, including Coca-Cola, Pepsi, Danone, and L'Occitane to give them recycled plastics. Danone said that it has a target to use 50% recycled plastics in its products by 2025.

Until environmentally workable alternative products to single-use plastics are found, the focus has to be on the safe, a) recycling, and b) disposal of plastic products.

How banks and companies can be part of the solution on plastics
The UN Sustainable Development Goal (SDG) 14 points to the

need to address the threat on marine life, and consequently on human health. This comes from a) increased ocean acidification, and b) pollution, especially plastics, which are not biodegradable. In order to simplify this goal, we would include "plastics management" as a metric to measure the health of water of the oceans and seas.

Banks have been engaged in the management of the plastics problem all over the world. Morgan Stanley's "Plastic Waste Resolution" is the best example we could find anywhere of what a bank can do about plastics. It is also one of the best examples of what banks can do in ESG. As the bank puts it: "Morgan Stanley is committed to tackling the growing global challenge of plastic waste in the environment. Through the capital markets and partnering with our clients and employees, we will prevent, reduce and remove 50 million metric tons of plastic waste from entering rivers, oceans, landscapes and landfills by 2030."

The Morgan Stanley plastic resolution can be a "working example" for banks of how to have a special ESG goal. This is because it has four functional elements. They include having:

a. a focused program,
b. a "measurable" target,
c. tackling a major ESG problem, and
d. being collaborative.

However, the program does not appear to be independently verified, which is a necessary element to ensure the credibility of the initiative.

Banks and companies can participate directly in, or finance one or more activities to control plastic pollution. These include, as mentioned earlier:

- Using and/or financing alternatives to plastics,
- Putting limits on the use of single-use plastics,
- Eliminating unnecessary packaging,
- Transitioning to return-and-reuse systems,
- Substituting virgin with recycled plastic or switching to other materials like paper,

- Capturing plastic waste effectively. This includes plastics on land and sea,
- Disposing of plastic waste,
- Recycling of plastic waste

AIR QUALITY MEASUREMENTS

Introduction:

Reducing air pollution is one of the major goals of ESG. It meets the two major criteria for inclusion as a goal. First, there is a major need to address air pollution. Second, the impact of investment in reducing air pollution can be very significant.

Air pollution is a major problem worldwide. It is also a problem in both developed and emerging countries. The World Health Organization, WHO, estimates that seven million people die each year from air pollution. Moreover, hundreds of millions of people have their life span curtailed because of air pollution. Their quality of life is also affected by air pollutants.

Air pollution is proven to be a major cause, or contribution to several health issues. Foremost among these are respiratory diseases including lung cancer. However, several other diseases are also caused to different degrees by air pollution. These include cancers, mainly in the respiratory tracts, and lung cancer in particular. Other cancers linked to air pollution include colon, stomach, kidney and bladder cancers. Air pollution is a cause also of circulatory system disfunctions, including strokes, high blood pressure, heart arrhythmia, coronary artery diseases, and heart attacks. They have also been linked to dementia and Parkinson disease.

The most encouraging information regarding air pollution is that remedial actions can be effective, and in a relatively short term. The success stories in reducing air pollution are many, and in different parts of the world. Possibly the most effective such measures taken by a country have been in the US. These have come as a result of the Clean Air Act of 1970, and its amendments. The Environmental Protection Agency

(EPA), which is the U.S. agency responsible for managing and tracking air de-pollution actions, has estimated that air in the U.S. has become 77% cleaner since then. Other U.S. studies that confirm these findings are from John Hopkins University and the American Lung Association. The economic benefits of clean air have permeated all sectors of the U.S. economy, including the private sector.

Other visible successes include the cleaning of the air in London, and in Istanbul. Those two large cities were known to have a heavy winter "smog" that came as a result of burning coal to generate heat (and power). The shift to less polluting fossil fuels, including the least polluting of them, natural gas, has resulted in both cities having generally good air quality.

These successes point out the need to consider taking "intermediate" measures before going all the way to "clean energy." There are clear benefits from going into a transition phase whereby air pollution is reduced, before reaching a phase where it is eliminated.

We will now look at the details of air pollutants both indoor and outdoors. These pollutants, and problems, can be tackled differently. Indoor pollution can be measured, and managed by banks and companies because it is under their control. However, outside air pollution is generally a public sector responsibility, and can be reduced by "macro-action," and regulations.

As a result of the measurement of indoor and outdoor air-pollutants, a bank or company can choose which pollutants are the most material, and where can there be the most significant impact from its own action to tackle them. A bank or company should aim at having acceptable air quality in its offices. A bank can also require the companies it finances to have acceptable air quality in their offices and plants.

Both indoor and outdoor air pollution should be monitored by a bank or company in our view. The idea of tracking only outside air pollution, as some standard setters do, is not the most effective methodology in our view. Both should be measured, and disclosed/reported, and tackled.

In all cases, when banks and companies measure these pollutants, and disclose them, they would be building their data base. They would also be building the "macro data bases" of the city, or country they belong to.

Finally, one should note that there are several readily available instruments that can measure the air pollutants commonly regarded as most harmful. Measurements of air pollution must be made, and if they have not been started, they need to be. What gets measured, gets managed, after all. We will now list he main air pollutants that need to be measured; first indoors, then outdoors.

Indoor Air Pollutants:

1. <u>PM2.5 Inhalable Particulate Matter:</u> These are very small particles measuring less than 2.5 micrometers. They are regarded as carcinogenic, and result in several other health hazards. Most developed countries have regulations to control these particulates.

   The particulates that are 2.5 or smaller are the most harmful. The smaller the particulates, the more hazardous they are. These are present both indoors and outdoors. They are also not a "single" pollutant, but are made of several small particles.

   PM 2.5 have been found in the brain, the respiratory system, the cardiovascular system, the renal system, and reproduction systems. Reduction in PM2.5 is known to lead quickly to fewer respiratory and circulatory problems in a community where pollution has been reduced.

2. <u>PM10: Particulate matter that are larger than 2.5 micrometers, but less than 10 micrometers</u> are inhalable, and can also result in health issues, especially in the long run. They aggravate asthma, and cause eye and throat irritation.

3. <u>CO_2: Carbon Dioxide:</u> Carbon dioxide is the "common variable" between two components of the "Environmental" goals of ESG:

Climate Change (as CO_2 is the main greenhouse gas), and Indoor Air quality.

CO_2 is primarily produced in offices and houses by unventilated closed spaces. The usually maximum acceptable is 1,500 ppm (parts per million). Outdoor CO_2 levels are usually around 400 ppm. The European Union limits acceptable CO_2 level to 3,500 ppm. CO_2 can harm human health in several ways.

4. TVOC: Total Volatile Organic Compounds: VOCs are harmful gases emitted in different households and offices. The sources are numerous. The most commonly found, and harmful indoor VOCs include formaldehyde, vinyl chloride, benzene, acetaldehyde, etc. Formaldehyde (CH20, or HCHO), which is an organic matter, is regarded as the "main" VOC.

    The sources of VOCs include various office equipment, supplies, printing, cleaning material, etc. There are several regulations in developed countries to limit the usage of products that emit VOC. Other regulations mandate the usage of products that give less VOC emissions. Europe (and California) lead in these regulations. There are many measurements of VOCs that are easily available.

5. Radon: Radon is one of the major in-house pollutants in more developed countries. Radon is measured, in picocuries politer of air (pCi/L). The hazardous levels are 4 pCi/L.

Outdoor Air Pollutants:

The EPA has limits on six pollutants in outdoor air. These are called the National Ambient Air Quality Standards (NAAQS). These are Ozone (O3), atmospheric particulate matter, lead (Pb), carbon monoxide (CO), sulfur oxides (SOx), and nitrogen oxides (NOx).

Nitrogen Dioxide (NO_2) can increase respiratory problems, including difficulty breathing and coughing. Ozone (ground level) can cause respiratory problems as well. The particulate matters are the same as the ones found indoors.

Detection methods are approved as Federal Reference Methods (FRMs). Newer ones, the Federal Equivalent Methods (FEMs) are based on newer technologies. The complete list of FRMs and FEMs are readily available on open sources.

As mentioned previously, several studies have calculated that reduction in outdoor air pollutants is possible, and mainly as a result of regulations. Millions of respiratory complications in the U.S. have reportedly been prevented or reduced since 1970 as a result of regulations. Pollution from transportation, mainly cars, trains and ships, have been reduced by 90% since then. Pollutants from manufacturing is estimated to have been cut by half. One of the most remarkable results is the reduction of 90% of lead pollutants since the elimination of leaded gas.

WASTE MANAGEMENT: THE CIRCULAR ECONOMY

Waste management meets the two criteria we have set to be an important ESG goal. First there is a need to address waste because this is a major problem in most countries in the world, but particularly so in emerging countries. Second, the efforts to address waste management problems can be effective.

We have already discussed the plastics waste problem in an earlier section of the chapter. Plastics constitute a major part of harmful waste produced by human activities. The principles to manage plastic waste can also be applied to the larger problem of managing all waste produced by human activities.

Waste management involves a) the collection of waste, and b) the disposal of waste. Waste management presents very large challenges in many emerging countries. This is mostly because it takes large investments, including capital, to manage waste. Moreover, waste management, including in developed countries, can many times be financially inefficient. The U.S., for example, has reportedly 26,000 waste collecting entities – which means the waste management process is possibly too fragmented to be economically efficient.

From an ESG perspective, waste management also includes processes that are not all environmentally friendly, especially in the disposal phase. The waste land-fills are major health risks for many cities in the emerging countries. They are also expensive. The burning of waste, which is another method for "managing waste" can also be a cause of environmental pollution, and GHG emissions. Even generating energy/power from burning waste can be harmful if not well managed.

There are several ways to manage waste in an environmentally friendly manner, and the technologies involved continue to develop rapidly. The most ambitious "comprehensive model" to handle waste management is what is referred to as the "circular economy." The circular economy aims at minimizing waste by redesigning many production processes. In its most advanced form, a circular economy would re-think the "supply-chain." Products are procured and designed to be recycled, and even re-used, and/or remade. Resources would also be used for much longer than they currently are.

Banks and companies have been, and can be involved in tackling waste management in environmentally friendly ways. First, banks and companies need to show that they are themselves managing the waste they generate in an environmentally friendly manner.

Second, banks need to encourage, and finance, their clients who are involved in waste management or who specialize in waste management. The banks need to ensure that a) waste is being managed, and b) that waste is being managed in an environmentally friendly way. Ultimately, c) banks can be actively involved in the design and implementation of the circular economy.

3

SOCIAL GOALS

INTRODUCTION

Social considerations for ESG are getting increasingly important because of three main reasons. First, there are very large needs in some areas in what is regarded as social goals in ESG. Second, investments and other positive actions in these areas can have high positive impacts, including significant financial returns. Third, the risks of not giving attention to these areas are relatively high.

The need for financial inclusion, for example, is very significant in many countries, especially in emerging ones. Relatively large sections of the populations of most emerging countries are underbanked. Even certain communities in some developed countries are also clearly un-derbanked. Investments in giving access to financial services would lift the income levels of these generally financially-disadvantaged persons, and increase economic growth rates. Moreover, these activities would be profitable for financial institutions if the associated financial risks are well-managed.

The social aspects of ESG have generally attracted more attention among international investors in emerging markets than environmental aspects. This is understandable because environmental aspects in many emerging countries pause lower global environmental risks (there are clear exceptions, such as deforestation in Brasil and Indonesia). Moreover, social aspects of an investment can have potentially high risks in emerging markets. Not least among these "social risks" are reputation risks, because of possible unacceptable practices in some countries. There are also the risks to the business invested in, because it would not meet one or more of the standards of the "Social" goals in ESG.

In addition to international investors, policy makers and regulators in the emerging countries focus on social aspects much more than on environmental ones. This is because the materiality and importance of some social aspects are generally high for the welfare and economic growth of these countries. This would all become clearer in the following discussion in this chapter of the main components of the social aspects of ESG.

The Social aspects of ESG generally overlap with many elements of Corporate Social Responsibility – CSR. CSR has been implemented by many companies and banks for decades. However, CSR is more limited in scope than the Social goals of ESG. CSR has also not been viewed as an investment "requirement," while ESG is increasingly becoming a requirement. Regulators moreover have not had CSR regulations, or reporting requirements, while they are moving to have guidelines and regulations for ESG.

CSR actions have been used to build the "brand" of a bank or company carrying them out, which is certainly acceptable. However, a more effective functional model would be one that links social responsibility actions, with financial returns. An ESG framework can indeed link social responsibility actions with financial returns - and in a systemic manner.

Because of the importance of the Social goals of ESG, especially in emerging markets, governments and international organizations can (and many do) have incentive programs to help make some of the social activities more financially viable. One of the most effective ways to do that is to have banks administer these programs. Banks would be in a good position to do that because they study the creditworthiness of these businesses, and would finance only viable ones. The viability of the business would include the incentives given to the banks, as they are "passed" to the businesses through subsidized financing, or similar government schemes.

There are many components that are included in the Social part of ESG. We are selecting a relatively small number of these that are among the most important for banks and companies to focus on, especially in the emerging markets.

The selected components have been chosen because of their relevance to emerging market banks in particular, and to their regulators. Some might give more focus on a particular aspect that is not covered here. However, the components that we are covering are the most commonly included in the Social pillar of ESG by different standard setters. Moreover, the more important social components we have selected to be implemented and measured are also among the UN's Sustainable Development Goals (SDG's).

We have selected ten components of the Social pillar of ESG. These have been selected, and are commonly included by most ESG standard setters as we have mentioned. We will expand the discussion of only some of these components in this chapter, because they would have a high impact if invested in and focused on. Metrics to measure these goals would be given in the discussion of each of these components. The main "social goals" that banks can focus on in ESG are the following.

1. Health: This conforms with SDG 3.
2. Gender Equality: This conforms with SDG 5.
3. Education / Training: This conforms with SDG 4.
4. Financial Inclusion: This conforms with SDGs 8, 1, 2.
5. Pay Equality / Pay Gap: This conforms with SDG 10.
6. Consumer Protection
7. Privacy
8. Community Support
9. Ethical Operations (Supply chain, and lending)
10. Stakeholders: Assessment of the Social Practices of Customers and Suppliers

We will discuss the first six of these indications in the following sections. Metrics to measure all ten indicators would be included in the ESG Reporting and Disclosure Metrics chapter of this book.

ESG: GENDER EQUALITY

Gender Equality has to be one of the main areas of attention of corporate and bank management. This is because it meets two main ESG eligibility criteria. First, it is an area where the need is very clear, and second, it is an area where action and/or investments can have very high impact/yield.

The fact more needs to be done on gender equality is reflected by numerous statistics. Females tend to have lower wages than males for the same jobs, females have lower employment rates, and females are less represented in higher management positions. These disparities are also more uneven among countries. Emerging countries have far larger gaps between the economic conditions of females and males than more developed countries.

And the female-male disparities in the emerging countries go deeper, and start earlier than in developed countries. This is best reflected in the education of females. Females have less university education than males in the emerging countries, and their high school dropout rates are also higher. Other indicators of female-male discrepancies include the fact that females are more prone to be abused.

Gender equality has come to mean more than "equality." It generally means,

1. Economic Equality: The treatment of women in the economic sphere as equal to men.
2. Inclusiveness: Allowing women to be included in all aspects of economic life.
3. Equal Pay: A woman needs to be paid a wage equal to a man doing the same work.

4. Diversity: The adequate inclusion of women in the workforce ensures diversity in its widest form.
5. Gender Financial Inclusiveness: Women need to be given equal access to financial services as men are.
6. Risk Management: Diversity reduces risks, and banks are about good risk management.

Gender equality's importance in the Social pillar of ESG is reflected in the fact it is one of the U.N.'s 17 Sustainability Development Goals (SDG's). It is goal 5 which aims to "achieve gender equality and empower all women and girls."

Ensuring gender equality is also important for the good functioning of a company or a bank for several reasons. These include the fact that the clients of the bank include women. Women are retail customers in their own right, or part of retail and small businesses. They are part of large corporations as well. If the bank is perceived as having good representation of women, then its female clients would be more comfortable dealing with it.

Moreover, any unequal treatment of females in the workplace, including in banks, has negative repercussions on the good functioning of the whole bank. This is because unequal treatment of those with qualifications, women or men, for whatever reason, leads to a decrease in the productivity of those who are discriminated against. This will also lead to a decrease in the productivity of the whole working force (or staff) of the bank, where part of the workforce would recognize that there are invisible barriers against their progress, and that advancement depends on factors other than merit.

Furthermore, job differentiation based on any factor other than qualifications and merit leads to the "introduction" of other differentiation criteria. This is because when one allows differentiation based on gender, one would allow differentiation based on other factors. These factors include race, national origin, religion, etc. But among these, the most important "level-playing-field" objective that needs to be achieved is gender-equality, because gender always affects half of any population, whether in a bank, in a corporation, or in society at large.

The metrics that can be used to measure and ensure gender equality can be:

1. Percentage of females in the bank or company workforce.
2. Women as a percentage in senior positions.
3. Number of females and males recruited and/or promoted, to executive and non-executive positions in the last year.
4. Average pay of females vs. average pay of males.
5. Percentage of females attending training during a year, compared to percentage of females in the work force.
6. Percentage of female clients (individual/retail) or women as a percentage of account holders.
7. Percentage of customer businesses controlled and/or owned by women.
8. Loans to women, or businesses controlled and/or owned, by women.
9. Women as a percentage of financial inclusion drives.
10. Performance Indicators (KPI's) on Gender equality for CEO, and senior executives.
11. Any independent "sounding" of staff needs to include the ability of females for advancement in the bank.

Almost all ESG social objectives, including gender-equality, are now positively encouraged. However, it is likely that many regulators would increasingly start to impose mandates about gender equality (or at least reporting on gender equality). The EU, for example, has clearly defined guidance on gender-equality.

FINANCIAL INCLUSION, AND FINANCIAL LITERACY

We will discuss in this section two related components of the "Social" pillar of ESG. These are financial inclusion, and financial literacy. We will mainly discuss the requirements of financial inclusion, then financial literacy.

Financial inclusion's most simple definition is the access of individual adults, and small businesses to accounts with financial institutions. The importance of having an account with a financial institution is that it helps an individual or a small business achieve one or more of the following objectives:

1. Security: Allows the account holder to keep money in a secure place with less risks of loss, theft, etc.
2. Payments: Improves the ability to receive and pay money, including making transfers.
3. Savings: Facilitates building savings.
4. Credit: Facilitates getting credit.
5. Financial Resilience: Improves the ability to get financing in emergencies.
6. Access to financial services in general.
7. Insurance: Improves the ability to get insurance services.
8. Securities: Improves the ability to invest in bonds and securities.
9. Gender Equality: Increases women's participation in the economy when they open their own accounts.
10. Convenience: Facilitates all transactions

These objectives are based mostly on definitions of the World Bank.

Financial inclusion has moreover major benefits to an economy as a whole, and not only to individuals and small businesses. The most important of these benefits is the addition of the "cash economy's" money supply into the banking system, which has direct impact on increasing economic growth and GDP. Financial inclusion also helps to bring the "informal economy" into the main-stream economy.

Financial inclusion enables a bank to broaden its client base and increase revenues. The bank can also make profits if it manages the process well.

Financial Inclusion helps to meet several goals among the UN's 17 Sustainable Development Goals, SDG's. These include SDG 1, No

Poverty; SDG 8, Decent Work and Economic Growth; and SDG 10, Reduced Inequalities.

Financial inclusion also overlaps with, and includes, several elements of other important elements of the "Social" pillar of ESG. These include a) gender equality, and b) financial education / knowledge.

Regulators have started to give guidelines to their banks on the importance of Financial Inclusion. Some regulators are actually mandating that the banks under their jurisdiction should have financial inclusion plans, and should report on the programs of implementation of these plans. A good example of this regulatory attention to financial inclusion is the mandate by the Central Bank of Egypt in 2020 to the banks it regulates to have plans to increase financial inclusion in Egypt, and report on the progress of these plans.

Technology is a major enabler of financial inclusion. Technology is not necessarily a pre-condition of financial inclusion, for banks can open accounts for low-income customers with basic technological requirements. However, technology is the most important enabler of financial inclusion. Technology can allow financial inclusion to be offered in scale. Put another way, technology allows financial inclusion to become scalable. Technology allows both a) the reach of a large number of customers, and b) lowering the costs of "mass production" of account-opening, and transaction processing. Mobile technology appears to be the most effective digital enabler of financial inclusion. Technology finally makes it easier for a bank to ensure that its financial inclusion efforts are profitable.

Financial literacy is as important as financial inclusion. Several studies have shown that financial literacy is important for the ability of an individual to use available financial products and services. This is in addition to his/her ability to manage his/her own finances. The need to improve financial literacy is a common problem in both developed as well as developing countries. The U.S. Financial Industry's Regulatory Authority (FINRA) estimates that more than 60% of Americans are in need to become more financially literate.

Many regulators in the emerging countries have programs to spread financial literacy among their populations. Some regulators require the banks they supervise to have financial literacy programs for their clients, and the regulators monitor the implementation of these programs. The best known global agency covering the subject is the OECD's International Network on Financial Education – INFE.

The metrics that banks can use to measure financial inclusion, and financial literacy, include:

1. Number of new accounts opened to individuals in lower income groups, and small businesses.
2. Number of products used by accounts of individuals in lower income groups, and small businesses (i.e. cross-selling of products).
3. Number of new accounts opened to women, especially women in lower income groups.
4. Efforts to improve financial knowledge. This is especially important because "financial education" is proven to increase financial inclusion.

EDUCATION/TRAINING

Banks and companies need to invest in training of their staff, and support education in their communities. This conforms with UN Sustainable Development Goal 4. SDG 4 calls to "Ensure inclusive and equitable quality education and promote lifelong learning opportunities for all."

The need for education is very clear in the emerging countries. School completion rates in most emerging countries are much lower than in developed ones. Moreover, education of girls tend to considerably lag the education of boys. Access to technology is also generally well behind basic needs among many schools in emerging markets.

A bank, or a company, can support education of staff in the organization itself, and of stakeholders outside the organization. A bank, or a company, needs to invest in education and/or training. Continuous training is needed for all staff of an organization, especially a bank, to keep up with the developments in the financial industry. It should be noted that attending most professional conferences can be considered training.

A bank or company need also to support education outside the organization. This can be through financing educational institutions. It can moreover be by direct support to students themselves at all levels. These are all education areas that can have the greatest impact if invested in, especially with adequate support and incentives from governments and international organizations.

The metrics that can be used to measure this needed education and training can include a) percentage of staff trained per year, b) hours of training per staff per year, c) financial investment/cost of training, d) investment in training compared to overall expense (or staff expenses), e) support for professional certifications of staff, such as in compliance, f) in-house training and outside training by hours and cost, g) e-training and classroom training breakdowns, and h) support for, or financing of, education institutions, and students.

CONSUMER PROTECTION

Consumers who deal with a bank must have their rights protected by bank regulators, and the bank itself. A bank's customer must also be able to have her/his complaints listened to, and addressed.

There are clear material needs for the "security/protection" of bank customers, as they are vulnerable to inside and outside infringement on their rights. Moreover, a bank should make it a priority to protect its stakeholders.

A bank should clearly disclose to its customers, at a minimum, their rights and responsibilities when engaging with the bank, or purchasing any of its products including:

- Opening an account,
- Fees and charges,
- Online banking,

- Fee changes,
- Lending conditions.

Most countries have their financial regulators define these financial consumer protection practices. However, to the extent they do not, or these regulations do not exist, a bank cannot be "ESG-compliant" if it does not have adequate consumer protection processes, and complaint mechanisms.

The protection of a bank's clients should include protection of their privacy. It should also involve having cybersecurity systems to protect them. There are extensive sources dealing with privacy and cybersecurity requirements, and we will therefore not cover them in detail here.

The metrics that can be used by a bank to measure this consumer-protection "social goal" follow. Some of these general consumer protection requirements overlap with Governance requirements, and some standard-setters actually include them under "governance" requirements:

1. Existence of systems to protect consumers,
2. Existence of complaint mechanisms for customers,
3. Implementation of systems to protect the privacy of customers and their data,
4. Implementation of cybersecurity systems to protect all stakeholders of a bank,
5. Implementation of systems to protect against fraud,
6. Implementation of processes to protect against money laundering,
7. Implementation of processes to protect against financing of terrorism.

ESG - HEALTH

Health considerations should be among the main Social Goals. The COVID-19 global pandemic has demonstrated the case for the need to make health issues a priority for any business, including banks. It has also shown that investments in health can have very significant impact on the well being of the stakeholders of a bank, and significant returns from these investments.

Most of the ESG and sustainability standard setters include health as one of the main metrics to measure, and a goal to pursue. There is a range of measures that a bank or company can take, and report on, to demonstrate that it is taking action on health.

Many banks and companies around the world have extensive reporting on the measures they have taken during the pandemic to protect their employees and customers. This is certainly worthwhile as the pandemic has been an unusual case, an "outlier," a "black swan," and it needed to be tackled with specific unusual measures.

The pandemic is also not the only health "special case" that has needed to be tackled with specific measures, although it is global in nature. There are many "local" special cases that come up and which need to be addressed in special ways. For example, a bank in California or Brazil might have taken special health measures during the wide forest fires in each of these "localities."

Health considerations overlap with other important ESG goals. The main areas are water availability and air quality. The goals a bank or company pursues in either of these areas are health goals, and can be regarded as such.

However general health measures are possibly more important to focus on, in addition to the "special" health occurrences, like pandemics and forest fires. The focus of some existing ESG standards is on "occupational health and hazards." This is certainly important, and should be covered by banks. However, the nature of the banking business which is mostly "office work," makes occupational hazards relatively limited. They are not the most "material" health issues for bank employees.

The more material health considerations in a banking organization, or any other business where office work is the main way of conducting business, is "health coverage." This means what health issues are covered.

A bank should disclose the health coverage plans it has for its employees. This is necessary because we were surprised to know that many health issues are not covered by some bank health plans, and more so in emerging markets banks. There are countries that have universal health coverage mandated by governments where extensive reporting does not become necessary. However, not all countries have universal health coverage.

The health coverage should cover all hospitalization costs – with the possibility that an employee must contribute a percentage of the cost. This contribution should ideally not exceed 10%. There should also be dental and eye coverage, maternity leave and childcare facilities.

The employees' access to adequate health services has been proven to affect morale and productivity. Overall health coverage also provides a sense of security to all staff of the organization.

Moreover, if health coverage is provided to all employees, productivity improves because there would be a sense of fairness in the organization. This comes from the fact that access to health is not dependent on an employee's salary, compensation, or net worth.

Equally important, a good health regime makes "preventive health" a priority. The areas covered include regular check-ups. The frequency of these check-ups would depend on different risk factors such as age and pre-existing conditions. Preventive measures also include encouragement of physical activities. Some banks have gyms on their premises, or subsidize enrolment in gyms.

Banks can factor in "occupational hazards" in their lending activities. It is sometimes crucial in some industries to ensure the borrower has proper coverage for its employees. Those industries include construction companies, and chemical plants. But this is "the second stage" of health coverage, after a bank covers its own staff.

The main health indicators a bank or company should oversee are mostly the following ones, and include those measures already discussed earlier in this section.

- A bank or company should have as comprehensive a health coverage for its employees as possible.

- The health coverage should cover hospitalization costs – with the possibility that an employee must contribute a percentage of the cost. This should ideally not exceed 10%. There should also be, if possible, dental and eye coverage, maternity leave and child care facilities.
- A good health regime makes "preventive health" a priority. The areas covered include regular check-ups.
- Banks or companies can factor in "occupational hazards" in their lending activities. It is sometimes crucial in some industries to ensure the borrower has proper coverage for its employees. Those industries include construction companies, and chemical plants.
- The organization/bank should ensure a healthy work-life balance. This balance is important for both the mental and physical health of employees.
- The organization/bank needs to measure absentee rates of employees to see whether there are health issues.
- It should be made clear to employees that mental well-being is as important as physical health.
- There should be reporting on working hours of employees. Excessive working hours have been shown to be counter-productive, and affect the physical and mental health of employees.

4

GOVERNANCE

INTRODUCTION

GOVERNANCE, THE THIRD PILLAR OF ESG, is important for the same reasons that make it important to pursue environmental and social goals, the other two pillars of ESG. The first reason is that there is a major need to have good governance, and the second is that there would be a high impact from very strong governance on achieving ESG goals.

Governance in ESG covers two interrelated domains. The first is governance of ESG management itself. The second is governance of the bank, or company, as a whole.

We will discuss in this chapter both the ESG governance criteria, and general corporate governance criteria of a bank or a company.

GOVERNANCE OF ESG

Governance of ESG is mainly about developing principles and practices for the governance and oversight of the environmental and social elements of ESG. These principles and practices have been developed by many standard setters. However, there are no generally acceptable standards for ESG governance, as is the case with the other standards covering ESG. Nevertheless, the general standards for ESG governance are easier to develop and agree on, because good governance principles and practices are firmly established. The best way to come up with ESG governance principles and practices is to base them on the general governance principles and practices.

We will discuss in this section the governance principles and practices of ESG, and list the most important indicators of these. The selection of these indicators and metrics is based mostly on their relevance to banks in the emerging markets. The sources for these indicators are several and include the papers by the Basel Committee on Banking Supervision, the WEF, the CCGG, SASB, GRI and others. The main measurements of ESG governance in a bank, or company, would be as follows:

1.   Business Strategy: It is important to include ESG considerations in the business strategy and plans of the bank or company. This is becoming increasingly necessary, because it is now abundantly clear that ESG is important in the creation of value for investors and shareholders, especially in the medium and long terms. The business strategy should also have a cost/benefit analysis to ensure that ESG activities envisaged and carried out do indeed create value to the bank, corporation, or organization.
     The ESG goals in the business strategy would cascade down to the different departments of the organization. These include the business lines, the risk management department, and human resources department (where ESG Key Performance Indicators, KPIs, would be included). It would be expected that many of the ESG goals of the bank and which are incorporated in the business strategy would be long term, by their very nature.

2.   Tone from the top: ESG would be regarded as important by all staff of the bank or company when the Board of Directors and CEO are seen as giving it importance. As an indicator of this, the attention the Board and CEO give ESG can be reflected in the business strategy.

3. Board composition: The board composition and talent mix should align with the business profile of the bank. The board mix should ideally have one or more directors with knowledge of ESG, and/or coming from disciplines aligned with ESG. These would include members with backgrounds in energy, education, engineering, small businesses etc. This would reflect the importance of ESG to the bank and organization as a whole. It would also ensure that the board's discussions of ESG are well informed.

    The board should also ensure that there is diversity in its composition, including proper representation of female directors.

4. Board Organization, and ESG-Specialized Executive: Board committees, and committee charters should define where ESG issues are discussed. This is because these ESG issues are now generally dispersed among many committees. The discussions of ESG issues should be a regular item on the agenda of one of the committees of the board which cover ESG issues.

    The ideal structure would have one board committee that would be responsible for, and dedicated to, ESG issues. The frequency of its meetings can be less than the frequency of the meetings of other committees, but its ESG "specialization" would ensure these goals are adequately pursued. However, it might not be necessary at an early stage to have a specialized ESG committee, especially in the smaller banks in the emerging countries.

    In addition to a specialized committee, the trend is now to have a specialized ESG manager in most of the large banks, and some of the medium sized banks in the emerging markets. This would be necessary because a specialized executive would give better focus to ESG in the bank. The most commonly used title of this executive is now the Chief Sustainability Officer or CSO.

5. Performance Evaluations: The board should ensure that the bank's senior executives who would be involved in ESG, have

part of their key performance indicators (KPIs) include achieving ESG goals. A KPI about ESG should be in the overall goals of the CEO and concerned senior executives. The weight of this KPI on ESG would depend on the particular bank or company, its business, and its size. It should be a minimum of 5% for ESG to be taken seriously. Some global banks already have ESG KPIs for their CEOs. Given that ESG goals are generally not financial in nature, a "balanced scorecard" approach would ensure that these goals are incorporated in the executives' performance assessments.

6. Disclosure: It is critical to have full reporting on the ESG activities of the bank or organization, as we have mentioned in the first chapter of this book. The ESG disclosures are important to all the stakeholders of the banks. The disclosures should include as much information as possible. The disclosed information would best be in a structured manner. It would cover all the metrics on all the ESG pillars, including governance.

   The ESG disclosures are the responsibility of the board, and senior management. ESG disclosures are best made through a separate stand-alone report. The practice by some banks to include ESG disclosures in the annual report takes away from the attention that ESG deserves.

7. Verification: The ESG report should be verified by an independent third party. The contents of the report should also be verified by the Internal Audit of the bank, as with all important activities of the bank. We will cover the need to have third party assurance in a specific chapter of this book.

8. ESG Plan: The bank should have an overall ESG plan. The plan should incorporate all ESG factors, to the extent possible. The ESG plan would be a basic one in the initial stage. The ESG plan's details and complexity would also depend on the size of the bank.

The ESG plan would list the main ESG objectives, the importance of each action that is to be taken, the responsibilities/priority of each executive involved in the process (i.e. who would do what), the resources necessary to achieve the objectives, and the time line to achieve these objectives.

The board, or senior management should ensure that the ESG plan is updated on a regular basis, at least annually. The board should also ensure that progress reports are being given to it, to help them monitor the good execution of the plan, or make changes in the plan as necessary. The accuracy of the progress reports should be verified by Internal Audit. Moreover, any disclosure or reporting of the ESG plan needs to be verified by an independent third party.

It is worth noting that the cost/benefit analysis of ESG activities in the ESG business strategy (and the plan) should take their long-term nature into consideration. The return on investment in ESG, for example, needs to be calculated on a long-term basis in some cases. The ESG plan should also include a risk/return analysis.

9. Risk Management: The risk management assessments, overseen by the board of directors, should include ESG factors. This should be at all risk management levels, from the overall enterprise risk management assessment (ERM), to operational risk, to the individual credit-risk assessment.
    A good risk management system would have risks measured and prioritized. This could be difficult in the case of ESG, especially because the financial measurement of the possible impact of ESG associated risks has its challenges. In all cases, ESG risks might impact the reputation of the bank, which means reputation risks are always present in ESG management. The disclosure process should include ESG risk materiality assessment, and risk prioritization.

The risks should be identified, and prioritized. A description of how they are to be mitigated, should then be made. These risks should then be monitored. The ESG risk assessment should cover the inherent risks, the control mitigating factors, and the residual risks. The risk appetite statement of the bank needs to include ESG risks, and their tolerance levels. These would be approved by the board as part of their approval of the overall Risk Appetite Statement of the bank.

It is necessary to reiterate here again that the complexity of this risk assessment would depend on the size of the bank, and the nature of its business. However, banks should start the ESG risk management/assessment process, even in a general format.

10. Materiality Assessment: The bank or company should have an assessment of those ESG areas or issues that are material to the bank or company. This is a necessary assessment in order to determine what ESG goals should be prioritized. The ESG framework cannot be a one-size-fits-all framework, because each bank or company has different economic, business and political settings it works within. Moreover each bank/company has different stakeholders, the ESG goals of a particular bank or a company need to be formulated based on the assessment of what is material to that bank or company and its stakeholders.

11. Proportionality: The Proportionality Principle should apply. This is especially true in the case of banks in the emerging countries where their size is generally far smaller than global banks. This means that the ESG goals that would be required of emerging markets banks would be smaller than what is required of larger global banks. On the other hand, the largest banks in an emerging country need to have larger ESG goals (and obligations) that smaller banks in that country.

For ease of reference the proportionality principle in corporate governance guidelines of the Basel Committee on Banking Supervision specifically states:

"*(Point 16) The implementation of these principles should be commensurate with the size, complexity, structure, economic significance, risk profile and business model of the bank and the group (if any) to which it belongs …*

12. Board Training: Board training is a Basel requirement. Board training and continuous education should include familiarization with ESG issues. ESG training/education of the board should be given priority because of the "novelty" of ESG issues to many banks and boards in the emerging countries.
    The reporting to the board should include reporting on ESG planning, and progress against these plans. Internal Audit should verify the accuracy of reports to the board. The board should ensure that ESG is an item for discussion in its regular meetings. This discussion of ESG matters should be on a quarterly basis at a minimum.

13. Code of Business Conduct: Code of business conduct is included in ESG under Governance goals by some standard-setters, or as part of Social goals by others. In either case, this is a significant factor that is important to international investors, mostly because of its impact on them from a reputational point of view. Business conduct includes both business ethics, and the lack of corruption and bribery in a company or bank.

14. Supply Chain Management: Supply chain management is another factor that is important to global investors. International investors, especially institutional investors, are coming under increasing pressure to ensure their suppliers in emerging countries do not use unacceptable practices in their home countries. These practices include child labor, for example. This is less of a risk for a bank itself in the emerging countries because their suppliers would not include these practices, by the nature of the banking business. However, a bank should have "vendor acceptance criteria" to ensure that their suppliers meet certain ethical criteria (as well as performance criteria).

The fourteen indicators selected above can measure and track a bank's adherence to good governance criteria in ESG management. We now turn to discuss the Corporate Governance criteria that all banks need to follow and that are broader in nature than governance of ESG on its own.

CORPORATE GOVERNANCE OF BANKS

It is a straight-forward simple task to "select" the general corporate governance criteria for banks. This is because these have already been formulated by the Basel Committee, and are generally accepted by all banks in the world, including the banks in emerging countries.

The foundational document for corporate governance for banks in the emerging countries is the guidelines on Corporate Governance issued by the Basel Committee on Banking Supervision.

We have included the more relevant principles for ESG in Basel's Corporate Governance Guidelines in a separate appendix of this book. The appendix would serve as a quick reference of the governance principles banks should follow.

GOVERNANCE APPENDIX

Selected Corporate Governance Principles From The Basel Committee's Guidelines

Basel's Corporate Governance guidelines are particularly aimed at banks, and this is the same target audience of this book. These Basel governance guidelines do not specifically cover governance related to Sustainability, and ESG, but they are necessary to ensure that a bank is well governed in all areas, and not only in ESG.

The following are relevant points and principles from the Basel Committee on Banking Supervision's Guidelines on Corporate

Governance that would be necessary to implement in any bank pursuing ESG goals.

*"(**Point 2**) The primary objective of corporate governance should be safeguarding stakeholders' interest in conformity with public interest on a sustainable basis."*

*"(**Point 3**) Corporate governance determines the allocation of authority and responsibilities by which the business and affairs of a bank are carried out by its board and senior management, including how they:*

- *Set the bank's strategy and objectives;*
- *Select and oversee personnel;*
- *Operate the bank's business on a day-to-day basis;*
- *Protect the interests of depositors, meet shareholder obligations, and take into account the interests of other recognised stakeholders;*
- *Align corporate culture, corporate activities and behaviour with the expectation that the bank will operate in a safe and sound manner, with integrity and in compliance with applicable laws and regulations; and*
- *Establish control functions"*

Risk Management is also a critical part of Governance: how the Board of a Bank, and its senior management determine risk tolerance, and oversee its implementation. Specifically:

*"(**Point 12**) Importantly, the FSB underscored the critical role of the board and the board risk committees in strengthening a bank's risk governance. This includes greater involvement in evaluating and promoting a strong risk culture in the organisation; establishing the organisation's risk appetite and conveying it through the risk appetite statement (RAS); and overseeing management's implementation of the risk appetite and overall governance framework."*

The accepted governance model is how the Board oversees the work of a three-lines of defence.

"**(Point 13)** Often referred to as the "three lines of defence," each of the three lines has an important role to play. The business line – the first line of defence – has "ownership" of risk, whereby it acknowledges and manages the risk that it incurs in conducting its activities. The risk management *function is responsible for further identifying, measuring, monitoring and reporting risk on an enterprise-wide basis as part of the second line of defence, independently from the first line of defence. The compliance function is also deemed part of the second line of defence. The internal audit function is charged with the third line of defence, conducting risk-based and general audits and reviews to provide assurance to the board that the overall governance framework, including the risk governance framework, is effective and that policies and processes are in place and consistently applied.*"

ESG has to stem from the Board. This is because:

"**(Point 14)** *The board should set the "tone at the top" and oversee management's role in fostering and maintaining a sound corporate and risk culture. Management should develop a written code of ethics or a code of conduct. Either code is intended to foster a culture of honesty and accountability to protect the interest of its customers and shareholders.*"

ESG Governance should be applicable in all jurisdictions **(Point 15)**

"**(Point 19)** *Recognising that different structural approaches to corporate governance exist across countries and that these structures evolve over time, this document encourages legislators, supervisors, banks and others to frequently review their practices so as to strengthen checks and balances and sound corporate governance under diverse structures. The application of corporate governance standards in any jurisdiction is naturally expected to be pursued in a manner consistent with applicable national laws, regulations and codes (eg taking into consideration the existence of oversight boards in some jurisdictions).*"

The proportionality principle should apply:

"**(Point 16)** *The implementation of these principles should be commensurate with the size, complexity, structure, economic significance, risk profile and business model of the bank and the group (if any) to which it belongs ...*

SIFIs are expected to have in place the corporate governance structure and practices commensurate with their role in and potential impact on national and global financial stability."

"Principle 1: Board's overall responsibilities

The board has overall responsibility for the bank, including approving and overseeing management's implementation of the bank's strategic objectives, governance framework and corporate culture."

"(Point 26) Accordingly, the board should:
Actively engage in the affairs of the bank and keep up with material changes in the bank's business and the external environment as well as act in a timely manner to protect the longterm interests of the bank;

- *Oversee the development of and approve the bank's business objectives and strategy and monitor their implementation;*
- *Play a lead role in establishing the bank's corporate culture and values;*
- *Oversee implementation of the bank's governance framework and periodically review that it remains appropriate in the light of material changes to the bank's size, complexity, geographical footprint, business strategy, markets and regulatory requirements;*
- *Establish, along with senior management and the CRO, the bank's risk appetite, taking into account the competitive and regulatory landscape and the bank's long-term interests, risk exposure and ability to manage risk effectively;*
- *Oversee the bank's adherence to the RAS, risk policy and risk limits;*
- *Approve the approach and oversee the implementation of key policies pertaining to the bank's capital adequacy assessment process, capital and liquidity plans, compliance policies and obligations, and the internal control system;*

- *Approve the annual financial statements and require a periodic independent review of critical areas;*
- *Oversee the bank's approach to compensation, including monitoring and reviewing executive compensation and assessing whether it is aligned with the bank's risk culture and risk appetite; and*

Oversee the integrity, independence and effectiveness of the bank's policies and procedures for whistleblowing."

*"(**Point 27**) The board should ensure that transactions with related parties (including internal group transactions) are reviewed to assess risk and are subject to appropriate restrictions (eg by requiring that such transactions be conducted on arm's length terms) and that corporate or business resources of the bank are not misappropriated or misapplied."*

*"(**Point 29**) A fundamental component of good governance is a corporate culture of reinforcing appropriate norms for responsible and ethical behaviour. These norms are especially critical in terms of a bank's risk awareness, risk-taking behaviour and risk management (ie the bank's "risk culture")."*

*"(**Point 32**) The bank's corporate values should recognise the critical importance of timely and frank discussion and escalation of problems to higher levels within the organisation.*

- *Employees should be encouraged and able to communicate, confidentially and without the risk of reprisal, legitimate concerns about illegal, unethical or questionable practices. This can be facilitated through a well communicated policy and adequate procedures and processes, consistent with national law, which allow employees to communicate material and bona fide concerns and observations of any violations in a confidential manner (eg whistleblower policy).*

This includes communicating material concerns to the bank's supervisor.

- *The board should have oversight of the whistleblowing policy mechanism and ensuring that senior management addresses legitimate issues that are raised. The board should take responsibility for ensuring that staff who raise concerns are protected from detrimental treatment or reprisals.*

The board should oversee and approve how and by whom legitimate material concerns shall be investigated and addressed by an objective independent internal or external body, senior management and/or the board itself."

"(Point 35) The board should take an active role in defining the risk appetite and ensuring its alignment with the bank's strategic, capital and financial plans and compensation practices. The bank's risk appetite should be clearly conveyed through an RAS that can be easily understood by all relevant parties: the board itself, senior management, bank employees and the supervisor."

"(Point 36) The bank's RAS should:

- *Include both quantitative and qualitative considerations;*
- *Establish the individual and aggregate level and types of risk that the bank is willing to assume in advance of and in order to achieve its business activities within its risk capacity;*
- *Define the boundaries and business considerations in accordance with which the bank is expected to operate when pursuing the business strategy; and*

Communicate the board's risk appetite effectively throughout the bank, linking it to daily operational decision-making and establishing the means to raise risk issues and strategic concerns across the bank."

"(Point 38) A risk governance framework should include well defined organisational responsibilities for risk management, typically referred to as the three lines of defence:

- *The business line;*
- *A risk management function and a compliance function independent from the first line of defence; and*

An internal audit function independent from the first and second lines of defence."

"Principle 2: Board qualifications and composition

Board members should be and remain qualified, individually and collectively, for their positions. They should understand their oversight and corporate governance role and be able to exercise sound, objective judgment about the affairs of the bank."

*"**(Point 48)** The board should be comprised of individuals with a balance of skills, diversity and expertise, who collectively possess the necessary qualifications commensurate with the size, complexity and risk profile of the bank."*

*"**(Point 49)** In assessing the collective suitability of the board, the following should be taken into account:*

- *Board members should have a range of knowledge and experience in relevant areas and have varied backgrounds to promote diversity of views. Relevant areas of competence may include, but are not limited to capital markets, financial analysis, financial stability issues, financial reporting, information technology, strategic planning, risk management, compensation, regulation, corporate governance and management skills;*
- *The board collectively should have a reasonable understanding of local, regional and, if appropriate, global economic and market forces and of the legal and regulatory environment. International experience, where relevant, should also be considered; and*

Individual board members' attitude should facilitate communication, collaboration and critical debate in the decision-making process"

*"(**Point 55**) In order to help board members acquire, maintain and enhance their knowledge and skills, and fulfil their responsibilities, the board should ensure that members participate in induction programmes and have access to ongoing training on relevant issues which may involve internal or external resources. The board should dedicate sufficient time, budget and other resources for this purpose, and draw on external expertise as needed. More extensive efforts should be made to train and keep updated those members with more limited financial, regulatory or risk-related experience."*

*"**Principle 3: Board's own structure and practices***

The board should define appropriate governance structures and practices for its own work, and put in place the means for such practices to be followed and periodically reviewed for ongoing effectiveness."

*"(**Point 63**) To increase efficiency and allow deeper focus in specific areas, a board may establish certain specialised board committees. The committees should be created and mandated by the full board. The number and nature of committees depend on many factors, including the size of the bank and its board, the nature of the business areas of the bank, and its risk profile."*

*"(**Point 72**) The risk committee of the board is responsible for advising the board on the bank's overall current and future risk appetite, overseeing senior management's implementation of the RAS, reporting on the state of risk culture in the bank, and interacting with and overseeing the CRO."*

*"(**Point 73**) The committee's work includes oversight of the strategies for capital and liquidity management as well as for all relevant risks of the bank, such as credit, market, operational and reputational risks, to ensure they are consistent with the stated risk appetite."*

*"(**Point 77**) Ethics and compliance committee: ensures that the bank has the appropriate means for promoting proper decision-making, due consideration*

of the risks to the bank's reputation, and compliance with laws, regulations and internal rules."

"Principle 4: Senior management

Under the direction and oversight of the board, senior management should carry out and manage the bank's activities in a manner consistent with the business strategy, risk appetite, remuneration and other policies approved by the board."

"(Point 89) *They should receive access to regular training to maintain and enhance their competencies and stay up to date on developments relevant to their areas of responsibility."*

"(Point 93) *Consistent with the direction given by the board, senior management should implement business strategies, risk management systems, risk culture, processes and controls for managing the risks – both financial and non-financial – to which the bank is exposed and concerning which it is responsible for complying with laws, regulations and internal policies.*

This includes comprehensive and independent risk management, compliance and audit functions as well as an effective overall system of internal controls. Senior management should recognise and respect the independent duties of the risk management, compliance and internal audit functions and should not interfere in their exercise of such duties."

"Principle 6: Risk management function

Banks should have an effective independent risk management function, under the direction of a chief risk officer (CRO), with sufficient stature, independence, resources and access to the board."

"(Point 105) *The independent risk management function is a key component of the bank's second line of defence. This function is responsible for overseeing risk-taking activities across the enterprise and should have authority* *within the organisation to do so. Key activities of the risk management function should include:*

- *Identifying material individual, aggregate and emerging risks;*
- *Assessing these risks and measuring the bank's exposure to them;*
- *Subject to the review and approval of the board, developing and implementing the enterprisewide risk governance framework, which includes the bank's risk culture, risk appetite and risk limits;*
- *Ongoing monitoring of the risk-taking activities and risk exposures in line with the board approved risk appetite, risk limits and corresponding capital or liquidity needs (ie capital planning);*
- *Establishing an early warning or trigger system for breaches of the bank's risk appetite or limits;*
- *Influencing and, when necessary, challenging decisions that give rise to material risk; and*

Reporting to senior management and the board or risk committee on all these items, including but not limited to proposing appropriate risk-mitigating actions."

*"**(Point 109)** The CRO is responsible for supporting the board in its engagement with and oversight of the development of the bank's risk appetite and RAS and for translating the risk appetite into a risk limits structure."*

*"**(Point 109)** The CRO's responsibilities also include managing and participating in key decision-making processes (eg strategic planning, capital and liquidity planning, new products and services, compensation design and operation)."*

*"**(Point 110)** While formal reporting lines may vary across banks, the CRO should report and have direct access to the board or its risk committee without impediment."*

*"**Principle 7** Risk identification, monitoring and controlling*

Risks should be identified, monitored and controlled on an ongoing bank-wide and individual entity basis. The sophistication of the bank's risk management and internal control infrastructure should keep pace with changes to the bank's risk profile, to the external risk landscape and in industry practice."

*"**(Point 113)** Risk identification should encompass all material risks to the bank, on- and off-balance sheet and on a group-wide, portfolio-wise and business-line level."*

*"**(Point 113)** The risk assessment process should include ongoing analysis of existing risks as well as the identification of new or emerging risks."*

*"**(Point 114)** Risk identification and measurement should include both quantitative and qualitative elements. Risk measurements should also include qualitative, bank-wide views of risk relative to the bank's external operating environment. Banks should also consider and evaluate harder-to-quantify risks, such as reputation risk."*

*"**(Point 117)** The degree of sophistication of the bank's risk management infrastructure – including, in particular, a sufficiently robust data infrastructure, data architecture and information technology infrastructure – should keep pace with developments such as balance sheet and revenue growth; increasing complexity of the bank's business, risk configuration or operating structure; geographical expansion; mergers and acquisitions; or the introduction of new products or business lines."*

*"**(Point 118)** Banks should have accurate internal and external data to be able to identify, assess and mitigate risk, make strategic business decisions and determine capital and liquidity adequacy. The board and senior management should give special attention to the quality, completeness and accuracy of the data used to make risk decisions. While tools such as external credit ratings or externally purchased risk models and data can be useful as inputs*

into a more comprehensive assessment, banks are ultimately responsible for the assessment of their risks."

"(Point 119) Risk measurement and modelling techniques should be used in addition to, but should not replace, qualitative risk analysis and monitoring."

"(Point 120) As part of its quantitative and qualitative analysis, the bank should utilise stress tests and scenario analyses to better understand potential risk exposures under a variety of adverse circumstances:

- *Internal stress tests should cover a range of scenarios based on reasonable assumptions regarding dependencies and correlations. Senior management should define and approve and, as applicable, the board should review and provide effective challenge to the scenarios that are used in the bank's risk analyses;*

Stress test programme results should be periodically reviewed with the board or its risk committee. Test results should be incorporated into the reviews of the risk appetite, the capital adequacy assessment process, the capital and liquidity planning processes, and budgets. They should also be linked to recovery and resolution planning. The risk management function should suggest if and what action is required based on results."

"(Point 122) In addition to identifying and measuring risk exposures, the risk management function should evaluate possible ways to mitigate these exposures. In some cases, the risk management function may direct that risk be reduced or hedged to limit exposure. In other cases, such as when there is a decision to accept or take risk that is beyond risk limits (ie on a temporary basis) or take risk that cannot be hedged or mitigated, the risk management function should report material exemptions to the board and monitor the positions to ensure that they remain within the bank's framework of limits and controls or within exception approval. Either approach may be appropriate depending on the issue at hand, provided that the independence of the risk management function is not compromised."

"Principle 8: Risk communication

*An effective risk governance framework requires robust commu-
nication within the bank about risk, both across the organisation
and through reporting to the board and senior management."*

*"(Point 129) Risk reporting to the board requires careful design in order
to convey bank-wide, individual portfolio and other risks in a concise and
meaningful manner. Reporting should accurately communicate risk exposures and results of stress tests or scenario analyses and should provoke a robust
discussion of, for example, the bank's current and prospective exposures (particularly under stressed scenarios), risk/return relationships and risk appetite
and limits. Reporting should also include information about the external
environment to identify market conditions and trends that may have an
impact on the bank's current or future risk profile."*

*"(Point 130) Risk reporting systems should be dynamic, comprehensive
and accurate, and should draw on a range of underlying assumptions. Risk
monitoring and reporting should not only occur at the disaggregated level
(including material risk residing in subsidiaries) but should also be aggregated to allow for a bank-wide or integrated perspective of risk exposures.
Risk reporting systems should be clear about any deficiencies or limitations in
risk estimates, as well as any significant embedded assumptions (eg regarding
risk dependencies or correlations)."*

"Principle 11: Compensation

*The bank's remuneration structure should support sound corpo-
rate governance and risk management."*

*"(Point 147) For employees in control functions (eg risk, compliance and
internal audit), remuneration should be determined independently of any
business line overseen, and performance measures should be based principally
on the achievement of their own objectives so as not to compromise their
independence."*

*"(**Point 148**) The remuneration structure should be in line with the business and risk strategy, objectives, values and long-term interests of the bank."*

*"(**Point 149**) Remuneration should reflect risk-taking and risk outcomes. Practices by which remuneration is paid for potential future revenues whose timing and likelihood remain uncertain should be carefully evaluated by means of both qualitative and quantitative key indicators. The remuneration framework should provide for variable remuneration to be adjusted to take into account the full range of risks, including breaches of risk appetite limits, internal procedures or legal requirements."*

*"**Principle 12: Disclosure and transparency***

The governance of the bank should be adequately transparent to its shareholders, depositors, other relevant stakeholders and market participants."

*"(**Point 151**) Transparency is consistent with sound and effective corporate governance. As emphasised in existing Committee guidance on bank transparency, it is difficult for shareholders, depositors, other relevant stakeholders and market participants to effectively monitor and properly hold the board and senior management accountable when there is insufficient transparency. The objective of transparency in the area of corporate governance is therefore to provide these parties with the information necessary to enable them to assess the effectiveness of the board and senior management in governing the bank.*

*"(**Point 152**) Although disclosure may be less detailed for non-listed banks, especially those that are wholly owned, these banks can nevertheless pose the same types of risk to the financial system as publicly traded banks through various activities, including their participation in payment systems and acceptance of retail deposits."*

*"(**Point 153**) All banks, even those for whom disclosure requirements may differ because they are non-listed, should disclose relevant and useful*

information that supports the key areas of corporate governance identified by the Committee. Such disclosure should be proportionate to the size, complexity, structure, economic significance and risk profile of the bank. At a minimum, banks should disclose annually the following information:

- *the recruitment approach for the selection of members of the board and for ensuring an appropriate diversity of skills, backgrounds and viewpoints; and*

whether the bank has set up board committees and the number of times key standing committees have met."

"(Point 154) In general, the bank should apply the disclosure and transparency section of the OECD principles. Accordingly, disclosure should include, but not be limited to, material information on the bank's objectives, organisational and governance structures and policies (in particular, the content of any corporate governance or remuneration code or policy and the process by which it is implemented), major share ownership and voting rights, and related party transactions. Relevant banks should appropriately disclose their incentive and compensation policy following the FSB principles related to compensation. In particular, an annual report on compensation should be disclosed to the public. It should include: the decision-making process used to determine the bank-wide compensation policy; the most important design characteristics of the compensation system, including the criteria used for performance measurement and risk adjustment; and aggregate quantitative information on remuneration. Measures that reflect the longer-term performance of the bank should also be presented."

"(Point 155) The bank should also disclose key points concerning its risk exposures and risk management strategies without breaching necessary confidentiality. When involved in material and complex or non-transparent activities, the bank should disclose adequate information on their purpose, strategies, structures, and related risks and controls."

*"(**Point 156**) Disclosure should be accurate, clear and presented such that shareholders, depositors, other relevant stakeholders and market participants can consult the information easily. Timely public disclosure is desirable on a bank's public website, in its annual and periodic financial reports, or by other appropriate means. It is good practice to have an annual corporate governance-specific and comprehensive statement in a clearly identifiable section of the annual report depending on the applicable financial reporting framework. All material developments that arise between regular reports should be disclosed to the bank supervisor and relevant stakeholders as required by law without undue delay."*

5

ASSURANCE

ESG REPORTING NEEDS TO BE VERIFIED

As we have mentioned in the introductory chapter of this book, the ESG reports of banks and companies would be credible only if there is independent assurance of what they are saying about their ESG activities and their products. ESG, and sustainability reports by the largest international banks and companies are now independently verified in order to provide assurance to investors. However, very few ESG reports in the emerging markets are independently verified.

Many regulators, including in the emerging countries, are seriously considering mandating that financial products or reports labeled "sustainable" or "ESG" should be verified, and assurance given by independent third parties. Mandating verification of ESG reports would be a necessary step to accompany any ESG guidelines issued by regulators of what is to be reported. Regulators are actually moving towards making some aspects of ESG reporting mandatory in the coming years as we have seen in earlier chapters. The European Union will make it obligatory to report major elements of ESG by end of 2022. Many regulators in the emerging countries, especially capital markets regulators, are also moving in this direction, and some have already issued guidelines on ESG reporting as we have also mentioned in earlier chapters.

Assurance of ESG reporting for a bank or company involves two parties. The first is the Internal Audit of the bank, and the second is a third independent specialist firm or consultant. The assurance, or verification must be of the ESG report, but it also would be needed for an ESG/green-labeled product, such as a bond.

A verification by a third party would reduce the risk of what is called "greenwashing." This is the mischaracterization of a product as green, while it might actually not be. Green washing should be detected and avoided. The best way to guard against greenwashing is to have independent verification of "green claims." Independent verification would also "go a long way towards addressing the concerns of investors and other stakeholders about the reliability of the sustainability information that companies report today," according to the EU.

Some financial products, including bonds, are becoming increasingly labeled "green," "blue," or "social." A bank or financial institution might market a bond as a "green bond," which indicates usually that the bond's proceeds would finance environmentally friendly projects. This "green labeling" would have to be verified by a third independent party, usually a consultant.

The same would apply to a "blue bond." A blue bond refers usually to a bond whose proceeds would finance projects that are good for water accessibility, or cleanliness, and/or good for cleaning the sea.

The independent verification can cover also reports prepared for rating agencies. Some rating agencies now rate products, and companies, according to how environmentally friendly they are. The Dow Jones Sustainability Index (DJSI) is one of these. It is part of the RobecoSAM Corporate Sustainability Assessment (CSA).

The need to have external verifiers of ESG reporting has been recommended by several international bodies. These include the UN Principles for Responsible Investment – UNPRIs. The European Union also supports independent verification of Green bonds by a specific standard: The EU Green Bond Standard "EUGBS." The same is recommended by the Climate Bond Initiative (CBI).

It should be underlined that the bank or company issuing an ESG report should itself draft the report, or marketing material for a "green" product. A consultant might be involved in advising on what the ESG plans should be, and what the ESG report should include, but this consultant should preferably not be the same one verifying the reports to avoid the perception of conflict of interest. The assurance work by a consultant should be independent of any advice on drafting an ESG report. The main responsibility of the consultant providing assurance should be to verify the accuracy of what is being reported.

The verification of what is being reported should be defined in a clear scope of work. It is preferable that the scope of work of the independent assurance given should be disclosed, to make the verification process transparent and credible.

The verification can generally be in two parts. The first is what can be termed as "Systems Assessment," and the second a "Data Verification."

A systems assessment would mainly cover the following:

- Existence of ESG plans and policies.
- Implementation status of ESG plans.
- Verification against a standard, if the report is using a specific standard. The fact the standards are not finalized means that the verification process would be limited to how the report generally conforms with the particular standard.
- The adequacy of the internal audit.
- Existence and implementation of governance systems.

Data Verification would include verification of all the measurements being reported. The data verification process would be based on a sample approach, and risk-based approach. The measurements to be verified would usually include:

- The accuracy of the ESG data being used and reported.
- The data on "Environmental" measurements. These include GHG emissions, water, and others.
- The data on "Social" measurements. These include financial inclusion, gender equality, etc.

The information to be verified would depend on the size of the bank, and what the bank is reporting.

THE STANDARDS FOR ASSURANCE REPORTS

There are existing standards that govern the verification processes, and these are being updated in the case of ESG. These standards depend on who is carrying out the verification exercise.

There are two parties needed to carry out verification of ESG reports, and/or ESG-labeled financial products and instruments. These parties, as we have mentioned earlier, are the Internal Audit of the bank itself, and the independent outside consultant carrying out the verification.

In the case of Internal Audit, Basel guidelines on Internal Audit provide a good foundation of what is to be done in the assurance of ESG activities, reports, and products of a bank.

Moreover, Basel's guidelines on Operational Risk can be used as guidelines on what would be expected from banks in the verification of their ESG reports. The "validation" parts of operational risks are not required in ESG, only the verification parts would be necessary. This would become more needed as ESG activities increase and become more sophisticated.

Specifically, Basel's verification guidelines for operational risks (which would apply for management of some ESG risks) state that "the depth and extent of the validation and verification efforts should be consistent with the materiality and complexity of the risk being managed."

In the case of outside consultants, the assurance would be based on International Standards on Assurance Engagements (ISAE) 3000. "Assurance Engagements other than Audits or Reviews of Historical Financial Information." In the particular case of Greenhouse Gases, it would be based on ISAE 3410 "Assurance Engagements on Greenhouse Gas Statements."

The assurance provided can be either a "limited" assurance, or a "reasonable" assurance. It is generally expected that regulators would first ask for a "limited" assurance, then move to require the more demanding "reasonable" assurance. A limited assurance has usually a "negative" statement. A limited opinion typically states that "nothing came to our attention to indicate that the information provided in the report is materially misstated."

The more comprehensive "reasonable" assurance has a positive statement. This would typically be "the information provided in the ESG report is reasonably stated based on the procedures we have carried out."

The EU is looking at introducing "a general EU-wide audit (assurance) requirement for reported sustainability information." This will help to ensure that reported information is accurate and reliable.

The European Commission would eventually allow its member states to open up the market for sustainability assurance services to so-called independent assurance services providers. These would be consulting companies other than the usual auditors of financial information, who would be allowed to work on providing assurance of sustainability information.

6

~~~~

REGULATORY INITIATIVES AND STANDARDS GOVERNING ESG

INTRODUCTION

REGULATORS OF THE FINANCIAL INDUSTRY are getting increasingly involved in each of the three elements of ESG – Environmental, Social,
and Governance. The regulators of capital markets have been ahead of
banking supervisors in the regulation of the ESG activities of the listed
companies (and banks) in the exchanges they supervise. This is mostly
because investments in ESG instruments have been the first ESG-labeled
instruments to come to the markets, and these investments involve capital markets more than banks.

Regulators and standard-setters have had so far two approaches to
issuing guidelines on ESG. The first approach is one that focuses on a
particular aspect of ESG. This is usually the first one, Environmental
goals, and specifically on issues and risks related to climate change.

The second approach, and in our opinion, more appropriate one,
is the comprehensive approach. The comprehensive approach covers all
three elements of ESG. The most notable practitioner of this comprehensive approach is the European Banking Authority, the EBA, as we
will see later in this chapter.

The comprehensive approach to ESG has started to be pursued in earnest by some emerging countries. This is particularly the case where the financial sector plays an important role in the economy. A noteworthy example of the comprehensive approach is what the United Arab Emirates stock exchanges have done. The two main exchanges in the UAE, the Abu Dhabi Securities Exchange (the ADX), and the Dubai Fund Market (DFM) have both issued comprehensive ESG guidelines in 2021.

The regulatory requirements involving ESG have focused mostly on disclosure requirements. However, they have recently come also to address risk management requirements. On risk management, regulators have been primarily concerned with their banks being resilient to risks associated with ESG. They have particularly focused on environmental risks, and more specially on climate risks. These risks have to be a) identified, b) measured, then c) managed; as with other regular banking risks.

Regulators are likely to ask banks to have two kinds of exercises in risk management. The first is scenario analysis, and the second is stress testing. We will cover these two exercises in more detail later in this chapter.

We will cover in this chapter what regulators are doing to address each of the three elements of ESG. Before doing that, however, it is important to note that some regulators are going first into a stage of "stock taking" of what exists among the banks they supervise. The second stage would be to issue guidelines. The third stage would be to have mandatory requirements for disclosures. They will also have requirements for risk management. This sequencing is not followed by all regulators. For example, the European Banking Authority, the EBA, has issued risk-management requirements ahead of disclosure requirements.

The "regulatory" measurements should cover both a) the architecture/structure in place. These are mostly the policies and staffing. They should also cover b) implementation or effectiveness of the overall architecture. This is a common methodology in regulatory compliance.

It is clear that bank supervisors need to have the skills necessary to supervise ESG related activities of the banks they supervise. Bank supervisors need to develop and/or acquire these skills because they are somehow different from the skills involved in "classical" banking supervision. The relatively "thin" ESG expertise in the emerging markets appears to be a main reason why the regulators in the emerging markets appear to be lagging behind in developing ESG guidelines for their banks.

Regulators are taking into account the standards being developed to cover ESG. These standards have been market-driven, and developed in most cases independently from the regulators. Regulatory guidelines being developed are in many cases themselves being guided by the standards that have been set. It is therefore necessary, before listing the regulatory initiatives on each of the three elements of ESG, to mention the main standards that are being developed to govern ESG.

THE DIFFERENT ESG STANDARDS

The different ESG standards that currently exist are not "commonly accepted standards," because they have been set by different standard-setters. They are also still in the development stage. There is recognition also that there is no agreement on the taxonomy. Green requirements (or definitions) in one country might be different from that in another. However, major developments in ESG standards are expected following the COP26 in November 2021. We will list below the main organizations that have set the existing standards, then go over the main ESG standard-setting initiatives that came out of COP26.

The main ESG standards have been set by the following organizations:

1. The Value Reporting Foundation: The Value Reporting Foundation is one of the main ESG standard setters focusing on ESG factors. It was created in June 2021 as a result of the merger of the Sustainability Accounting Standards Board (SASB), and the International Integrated Reporting Council (IIRC).

   The Sustainability Accounting Standards Board (SASB), is a non-profit U.S. – based organization. SASB creates and disseminates accounting standards that reporting issuers can use to disclose material sustainability factors in filings with the Securities and Exchange Commission. SASB has developed provisional standards for more than 80 industries in 10 sectors. SASB has also developed a "Materiality Map" that helps users identify SASB disclosure topics on an industry-by-industry basis and compare the potential materiality of various sustainability factors across different industries and sectors.

The International Integrated Reporting Council (IIRC) is a group from the corporate, investment, accounting, securities, regulatory, academic, and standard-setting and civil society that has created the Integrated Reporting framework. The Framework aims to provide material information about an organization's strategy, governance, performance and prospects.

2.   The Global Reporting Initiative (GRI): The GRI is an international, not-for-profit organization that has developed comprehensive environmental, social, and governance guidelines. The GRI's sustainability reporting guidelines are among the more widely used ESG guidelines.

3.   The World Economic Forum (WEF): The World Economic Forum has led another major global ESG standards initiative. These have been developed by the World Economic Forum in cooperation with the "Big Four" auditing firms. This has been driven under the leadership of Bank of America.

4.   CDP (formerly the Carbon Disclosure Project): The CDP is a global not-for-profit organization headquartered in London. The CDP collects standardized climate change, water and forest information from some of the world's largest listed companies through annual questionnaires sent on behalf of institutional investors that endorse them as 'CDP signatories'. This standardized information allows banks and companies to be transparent about environmental risks.

The main standard setting initiatives that came out of COP26 were announced by the IFRS Foundation. They include:

-   The formation of a new International Sustainability Standards Board (ISSB) "to develop a comprehensive global baseline sustainability disclosure standards to meet investors' information needs";
-   Consolidation of the Climate Disclosure Standards Board and the Value Reporting Foundation by June 2022;
-   The general disclosure standards would be based on work by representatives of the CDSB, the International Accounting Standards Board (IASB), the Financial Stability Board's Task Force on Climate-related Financial Disclosures (TCFD), the VRF and the World Economic Forum (Forum), supported by the International Organization of Securities Commissions (IOSCO).

REGULATORS AND ENVIRONMENTAL GOALS: THE E OF ESG

Regulators have been increasingly focusing on the environmental part of ESG, and specifically on climate change. The second part of environmental risks, the risks to the ecosystem, is not yet being addressed by regulators in the same systemic way as the risks of climate change.

It is important here to list the main international regulatory initiatives on Environmental goals, and what the regulatory expectations are in this space.

The Financial Stability Board, acting for the G20 Finance Ministers and Central Bank Governors, established the Task Force on Climate-Related Financial Disclosures (TCFD) in 2015. The TCFD is doing what its name stands for: develop recommendations for more effective climate-related disclosures.

Another major regulatory initiative related to management of climate change was the establishment of the NGFS – the Network of

Central Banks and Supervisors for Greening the Financial System. It was established in December 2017 as a group of the willing "to share best practices and contribute to the development of environment and climate risk management in the financial sector, and to mobilize mainstream finance to support the transition towards a sustainable economy."

The NGFS had originally 7 founding members, but has grown ten fold in three years. The NGFS now includes regulators from countries that are responsible for around 70% of GHG emissions – hence its work can be effective in containing the related risks.

Regulators are likely to ask banks to have two kinds of exercises – the first is scenario analysis, and the second is stress testing. Scenario analysis would look at different scenarios, and would focus on the 30 year time frame to achieve net zero. It will include negative outcomes but might include positive outcomes as well.

Stress testing would be an exercise that would test a bank's resilience against a specific climate shock. It would include the "tail-risk," "black-swan" – and thinking of the unthinkable. There are currently some larger banks who are carrying out climate risk stress tests. This stress testing is however clearly not yet the norm.

The TCFD recommendations have gained wide acceptance, including among regulators. The Bank of England wants the TCFD requirements to become mandatory by 2025. The TCFD has separated climate-related risks into two main categories a) transition risks, and b) physical risks.

Transition risks are the "risks related to the transition to a lower carbon economy." The TCFD further separates transition risks into four subcategories, and includes what the potential financial impact may be from each of these risks. These four potential transition risk sub-categories are a) policy and legal risks, b) technology risk, c) market risk and d) reputation risk.

Similarly the TCFD separates physical risks into two categories: a) acute risks, b) chronic risks. Acute physical risks refer to "those risks that are event-driven, including increased severity of extreme weather events, such as cyclones, hurricanes, or floods."

Chronic physical risks refer to "longer-term shifts in climate patterns (e.g., sustained higher temperatures) that may cause sea level rise or chronic heat waves." The TCFD gives specific examples of risks related to both categories of physical risks.

The TCFD's recommendations serve to encourage organizations to evaluate and disclose, as part of their annual financial filing preparation and reporting processes, the climate-related risks and opportunities that are most pertinent to their business activities.

The most comprehensive guidance and discussion of ESG risks for financial institutions has been published by the European Banking Authority (EBA) in June 2021. It is called "the EBA report on management and supervision of ESG risks for credit institutions and investment firms."

The EBA report covers the risks associated with all three ESG categories: environmental social and governance risks. It is worth noting that the EBA follows the categorization of the TCFD in separating environmental risks into physical risks, and transition risks.

The EBA's 2021 report on risk management in financial institutions, and how they are to be supervised by regulators in the EU, follows the earlier general plan the EBA published in December 2019. That general plan, entitled "EBA Action Plan on Sustainable Finance" gives the timeline and milestones of the EBA's work on Sustainable Finance.

The EBA plans to have extensive disclosure requirements from its supervised financial institutions. These would be on a "sequential approach." Certain disclosures are expected in June 2024. These would be scope 3 emissions and the proposed Green Asset Ratio (GAR).

REGULATORS AND SOCIAL GOALS: THE S OF ESG

The Social goals have been getting the least attention of regulators among the three elements of ESG. Regulators can have transformational change in this area, especially in the emerging/developing countries. This is because regulators, as we have been mentioning throughout this book, are leaders of change in the financial industries they supervise in the developing countries. One clear example of this is the major strides banks have made in compliance (mainly in anti-money laundering, and counter finance of terrorism). Regulators are also the transmitters of global regulations (and in many cases, progress) in their financial industries in the emerging countries.

The areas worth noting and which regulators in developing markets have been increasingly focusing on are a) financial inclusion, b) gender equality, and c) education.

Regulators in the developing countries are giving increasing attention to financial inclusion because of the clear impact financial inclusion has on society as a whole, and because their governments are also giving financial inclusion a high priority. There has also been mounting evidence that banks that expand their client base to include low-income groups who do not use financial services, would find these clients financially profitable. This is also basically common sense: the larger the client base, the larger the revenues. Earnings themselves can also be larger, if the costs are well managed.

Some regulators in the emerging countries are actually mandating that the banks they supervise have financial inclusion goals. The supervisors would then monitor the implementation of these plans. One good example of the involvement of banking supervisors in financial inclusion is Egypt. The regulator in Egypt, the Central Bank, felt it necessary to push banks to pursue financial inclusion. They obviously felt that what could have been a "voluntary activity" needed to be pursued with involuntary measures to make it materialize.

Two other areas where banking supervisors give attention to among the banks they supervise are gender-equality and education. Gender equality, in all its aspects (including representation, and equal pay) is sometimes covered under governance principles (and not only social ones). Education is generally covered by supervisors in their monitoring of the training and qualifications of the staff of banks and financial institutions they supervise.

Supervisors in the emerging markets are doing a lot to have their banks pursue social goals. However, it is also clear that they can do much more to lead the banks and financial institutions they supervise to pursue the Social goals of ESG more comprehensively, and more effectively.

REGULATORS AND GOVERNANCE: THE G OF ESG

Banking supervisors, and capital markets regulators have been mandating for decades that their supervised banks and companies pursue corporate governance. The regulations covering governance are the most "mature" among all regulations covering ESG, both for banks and companies. This is because it has now been firmly established that governance is the "mother" of all good management, and risk-control practices.

Corporate governance requirements for banks are well defined by the Basel Committee as we have seen in an earlier chapter. Banking supervisors can simply extend their supervision of good corporate governance to also cover supervision of governance of ESG activities of banks. The governance requirements of ESG have been covered as well in the chapter on governance.

Supervisors are obliged according to the Basel Committee's requirements to oversee good governance in the banks they supervise. We will go quickly over what supervisors can do about governance of ESG, based on what the Corporate Governance foundational document of the Basel Committee stipulates.

The specific points in the Corporate Governance Guidelines of the Basel Committee which are the basis for regulations and supervision of ESG include the following points:

(Point 21)

"Supervisors should provide guidance for and supervise corporate governance at banks, including through comprehensive evaluations and regular interaction with boards and senior management, should require improvement and remedial action as necessary, and should share information on corporate governance with other supervisors."

(Point 157) *"The board and senior management are primarily responsible for the governance of the bank, and supervisors should assess their performance in this regard."*

(Point 158) *"Supervisors should establish guidance or rules requiring banks to have robust corporate governance policies and practices. Such guidance is especially important where national laws, regulations, codes or listing requirements regarding corporate governance are not sufficiently robust to address the unique corporate governance needs of banks. Regulatory guidance should address, among other things, expectations for checks and balances and a clear allocation of responsibilities, accountability and transparency among the members of the board and senior management and within the bank. In addition to guidance or rules, where appropriate, supervisors should also share industry best practices regarding corporate governance with the banks they supervise."*

(Point 159) *"Supervisors should have processes in place to fully evaluate a bank's corporate governance. The evaluations should include regular communication with a bank's board of directors, senior management, those responsible for the risk, compliance and internal audit functions, and external auditors."*

(Point 160) *"Supervisors should evaluate whether the board and senior management have processes in place for the oversight of the bank's strategic objectives, including risk appetite, financial performance, capital adequacy, capital planning, liquidity, risk profile and risk culture, controls, compensation practices, and the selection and evaluation of management. Supervisors should focus particular attention on the oversight of the risk management, compliance and internal audit functions."*

(Point 161) *"Supervisors should evaluate the processes and criteria used by banks in the selection of board members and senior management and, as they judge necessary, obtain information about the expertise and character of board members and senior management. The individual and collective* *suitability of board members and senior management should be subject to ongoing attention by supervisors."*

(Point 162) *"As part of their evaluation of the overall corporate governance in a bank, supervisors should also endeavour to assess the governance effectiveness of the board and senior management, especially with respect to the risk culture of the bank. This includes consideration, such as how the "tone at the top" and the cultural values of the bank are communicated and put into practice, and how potential serious problems are identified and addressed throughout the organisation. Supervisory staff should have the necessary skills to evaluate these issues and arrive at the complex judgments involved in assessing governance effectiveness."*

(Point 164) *"Supervisors should also provide insights to the bank on its operations relative to its peers, market developments and emerging systemic risks."*

7

~~

A BALANCED APPROACH TO ACHIEVING ENVIRONMENTAL, SOCIAL AND GOVERNANCE GOALS

WE ARE MAKING THE ARGUMENT in this book that banks and companies, especially those in emerging countries, need to have a balanced approach in pursuing ESG goals.

One main reason for having a balanced approach to ESG is that it is the most effective way to implement ESG by banks and companies in the emerging countries, as we would show in this chapter. A balanced approach is also the most suitable approach for banks in the emerging markets to take.

We also believe that having a balanced approach would incentivize banks in emerging counties to plan and implement ESG programs, and report on these ESG programs as they implement them. The call for a balanced approach to ESG is a call for action to the banks in the emerging countries to fully engage in the global ESG efforts.

The need for banks in the emerging markets to act is clear from the 2020-2021 comprehensive survey that Amdeya carried out about the implementation of ESG by 701 banks in 41 emerging countries. The Amdeya survey found out that only 32% of banks in the emerging countries reported on ESG in one way or another. The non-disclosure of ESG activities would indicate that those who do not report on ESG actually do not have ESG programs.

Yet banks in the emerging countries can do a lot on ESG, because these banks have significant roles in their economies. The role of banks in emerging countries is generally larger in their economies, in relative terms, than the role of banks in the developed economies.

We will now define what we mean by a "balanced approach," and why a balanced approach is the most effective way for banks and companies in the emerging countries to set and achieve ESG goals. Many of these points have already been covered in earlier chapters in more detail.

1. A balanced approach to ESG should recognize, first, that addressing climate change is the most important goal among ESG goals. To have an effective balanced approach to ESG, one has to first recognize that reversing climate change as the main goal for ESG.

    Climate change is certainly important. It is an existential issue for humanity. It should be considered as the most important among ESG goals. As mentioned in earlier chapters, carbon dioxide and other Green House Gases (GHGs) emissions are increasing global warming. This in turn is increasing the frequency of severe weather, ocean levels, desertification and forest fires, among others. These and other negative repercussions will need to be tackled, and the trends reversed. The Paris climate accord aims to have the world achieving net-zero GHG emissions by 2050. This would be achieved by several measures that would be taken by international organizations and individual countries. Each country would work through its public and private sectors to achieve these goals. Banks and companies in each country would be expected to play a major role in these global and country endeavors.

2. A balanced approach necessitates that the approach is <u>comprehensive</u>. A balanced approach means that the selected ESG objectives should include elements from all three broad goals

of ESG: Environmental objectives, Social objectives, and Governance objectives.

A balanced approach to ESG would take into consideration all the elements of ESG, and not only a single part of it. The need to balance all environmental, social and governance considerations when setting objectives and implementing them reflects the diversity of interests of the many stakeholders a bank has in an economy. These stakeholders include investors, shareholders, clients, employees, suppliers, international financial institutions, rating agencies, and regulators.

3. A balanced approach that is comprehensive and includes all aspects of ESG would satisfy the increasing demands of one of the most important stakeholders of a bank or a company, the international investors. International investors want different ESG factors to be taken into consideration in the activities of the bank they deal with and companies they invest in. Large international banks are increasingly asking, and expecting the smaller banks in the emerging markets to advise them on what they are doing about ESG goals. This is because the larger banks are themselves being asked to report on what they are doing about ESG goals. The smaller banks are basically "clients" of the large international banks, and banks are expected to ensure their clients take into consideration the concerns of their stakeholders.

The fact investors are looking for all elements of ESG in investments is reflected in a 2019 survey of global fund institutes by BNY Mellon. The survey showed that the top five <u>increases</u> in inquiries from investors were the following:

- 51% Board composition and structure (G)
- 42% Diversity and inclusion (S)
- 35% Climate change and carbon emissions (E)
- 34% Executive compensation (G)
- 31% Energy Efficiency (E)

4. The fact banks and companies can approach ESG as a "balanced package" including all three elements, E, S, and G, can be viewed as an opportunity for them. It is the opportunity not to be tied to, or cornered-in, only one set of goals. The fact ESG bundles together Environmental, Social, and Governance goals allows one to choose what is more material to the company, based on its own criteria. There is less "imposition" of certain goals, and there is more freedom of choice of goals.

5. A balanced approach means that banks can be <u>selective</u> of the main objectives/goals they choose to pursue. The need to have a selective approach to ESG goals is based on the need to select objectives that are material, relevant, practical, implementable, and have the highest impact for the stakeholders and community the bank serves. This is what is meant by the "materiality" principle. However, the selected goals (and measurements) need to be in all three ESG components as mentioned earlier, notwithstanding that there can be a "focus" on certain objectives.

6. A balanced, comprehensive approach that includes all aspects of ESG conforms with the U.N.'s approach. The U.N. has 17 SDGs – the Sustainable Development Goals. ESG goals overlap with the U.N.'s Sustainable Development Goals, although the SDGs are more comprehensive than ESG goals. The point is that the U.N.'s SDG goals are a "package" of goals, as ESG goals should be.

7. A balanced approach would demonstrate to emerging countries, and their banks, that it is in their interest to pursue environmental goals. This is because environmental goals to address climate change would be regarded as only part of the goals to be pursued in an overall ESG program.

   It is necessary to make this point because some in the emerging countries, and their banks, appear to have a lukewarm view towards working to address climate change. They say they can do little about it because emerging countries have economies that produce less carbon dioxide than developed countries. This is because most of these economies are relatively small. Emerging countries also emit less carbon dioxide than "richer" countries per capita because they have lower income per capita than developed countries. In other words, a rich person has a larger carbon footprint than a financially disadvantaged person. This is notwithstanding that those who make these arguments recognize that all countries are impacted by climate change to differing degrees.

Most developing and emerging countries have a vested interest in reversing climate change. Many emerging countries have been at "the receiving end" of the worst impact of climate change. Some countries in sub-Saharan Africa face existential threats because of increased desertification. Others like Bangladesh, face threats from rising seas. The Gulf oil producing countries are actually being impacted heavily by climate change, with average temperatures rising, and rain becoming less frequent. This is why we see some of the Gulf oil producers, such as Abu Dhabi, among the most aggressive in pursuing actions to reverse climate change.

8. A balanced approach would have each country, company and/or bank work to tackle the climate change problem according to its size, and the extent to which it produces GHGs.
    Each country, large or small, rich or poor, must have a role in the global campaign to reverse climate change – precisely because this is a global problem. However, the proportionality principle would have each country tackle environmental problems according to its capacity. The same principle would apply to banks and companies; each would work according to its capacity.

9. Within Environmental considerations, achieving net-zero emissions is itself a "balancing-act." The world cannot achieve

net-zero, and is not aiming to achieve net-zero, by eliminating carbon and GHG emissions. The idea is to have a new "energy mix" by 2050, and take other measures to achieve net-zero. Clean energy would continue to grow exponentially. Fossil-fuel efficiencies would continue to increase, which would help reduce the overall emissions. Moreover, other activities, including carbon capture usage, and storage (CCUS) need to increase significantly. But most important among these balancing factors in achieving a new energy mix is the production of "alternative energy" to fossil fuel that would produce no carbon dioxide (such as solar). The combination of all these efforts, and others, would achieve global net-zero emissions by 2050.

We have devoted the chapter on "Environmental Goals: Climate Change" to the efforts to change the energy mix, and carbon capture, and what banks and companies are expected to do to achieve these goals.

10. A balanced approach by banks should take into consideration the impact from the activities they finance, and not only from their own activities. A balanced approach would have the banks factor into their ESG plans the environmental and social activities they finance – and Governance they ask for from their clients.

    These financed ESG activities include Scope 3 emissions in the environment. Banks, including in the emerging markets, would find that the Scope 3 emissions of their clients are significant, especially compared to the bank's own emissions. They would need accordingly to try to measure them and/or have their clients measure them. They would then need their emissions to be disclosed.

11. A balanced approach to ESG involves balancing requirements within the Environmental component of ESG. The focus has been predominantly on climate change, and there is good reason for that because climate change is the most "existential"

environmental challenge to the planet as we have mentioned. Yet there are other environmental challenges that are more pressing in many emerging economies. These challenges have been discussed earlier, and include water availability and cleanliness, plastic pollution, air pollution, and waste management. It makes sense, for example, to focus resources on getting water in some countries rather than on reducing their relatively small carbon emissions.

12. A balanced approach would allow some emerging countries to focus on the non-environmental elements of ESG, specifically Social and Governance goals. The return on investment in Social and/or Governance would be higher than their investment in E for some of these countries.

    The Social and Governance needs of emerging countries are vitally important for the progress of these countries. In many cases, they are matters of survival. They include education, financial inclusion, gender equality, employment, and good governance. Working towards progress on gender equality in most emerging countries, for example, is more pressing than in more developed economies. This is because the disparities between the economic and social status of females, compared to males, are considerably worse than those in developed economies.

13. A balanced approach necessitates taking the overall impact on ESG of certain ESG actions. One reason a balanced approach is warranted is that the data given on one ESG element cannot sometimes be separated/insulated from other factors. For example in plastic management, some processes for plastic removal might be energy-intensive, and emit a lot of CO_2 and other GHGs. A balanced assessment of the process in this case would find that the environment might be better off not removing plastics if this involves using an energy-inefficient thermal process. Another example is in water desalination. In this case, a balanced approach to ESG needs to take into account both the

carbon emissions from water desalination processes, and the benefits of having water available to communities in need of water. As mentioned earlier, clean water availability is a high priority goal for all communities, rich and poor. The need for water outbalances the possible need to use fossil fuel in its production in some extreme cases.

One can argue that, ideally there should be an "offset program" to allow the generation of clean water through fossil fuels to offset the emission of carbon dioxide. This is because the lack of fresh water is as serious an issue for certain countries and communities as climate change is.

14. A balanced approach to ESG would have developed countries focus more on ensuring that all countries, including emerging countries, get involved in the efforts to tackle ESG challenges - including climate change. This is recognized in the Paris Accord, and has been underlined in COP26, which was held in late 2021. Developed countries have made specific pledges in COP26 to help emerging countries on ESG.
The more advanced economies have an interest in helping many emerging countries tackle the challenges of climate change. This is because climate change will affect the very livelihood, if not survival, of many in the emerging countries – and these would seek refuge in the richer countries. To stem the already rising waves of immigration to the richer countries, like the move from Africa to Europe, it is only logical to help those poorer countries develop their "defences" against climate change.

Helping build defences of some emerging countries against climate change includes helping to strengthen the Social and Governance pillars of ESG, from education, to water availability, to gender equality to good governance. And this can also include helping these economies, many of whom are starved for energy, develop alternative energy to fossil fuel. Some of the best investments in ESG from developed economies, in terms of returns, could be investments in renewable energy in emerging countries.

The assistance from the developed economies to emerging economies could mostly come through the banks of the emerging economies. This is because banks in most emerging countries play a major role in the economies of these countries, and it would be most effective to channel these investments through the banks of the emerging economies.

15. A balanced approach to ESG would take into consideration the business aspects of ESG. To ensure ESG becomes embedded in the business of a company or bank, it is important that ESG should not be seen as an expense, or cost. ESG should not be a "cost center." To the extent possible, there should be revenues associated with ESG activities. These revenues would include financial-inclusiveness activities, financing alternative energy (solar, wind, ...), financing health businesses, education, women's owned business, and all activities that would help meet ESG targets. A bank can "allocate" these revenues to an ESG profit center.
Moreover, there can be cost reduction associated with ESG. These can be the result of government tax-credits for some aspects of ESG programs. On the revenue side, governments can have other incentives to encourage ESG.

The "Carbon Markets" being pursued, and the actual "carbon-trading" that already exists (although in small dimensions) would be most effective if it is monetized as much as possible. This market should not be viewed as the equivalent of "barter-trade." Active carbon markets can lead to significant revenues. Carbon Capture Usage and Storage (CCUS) activities are part of the activities that can be included in carbon markets.

16. A balanced approach to ESG recognizes that there will <u>be a transition phase until ESG goals are met</u>. Managing the transition phase has many elements of crises management. This is because, in the case of the environment, the unfortunate truth is that climate change, particularly global warming, is very likely going to get worse in the coming years, before the current worsening trends are reversed. In other words, it is likely that things will get worse before they get better. Businesses and banks all over the world will have to deal with this worsening phase. This transition phase is going to take anywhere from 10 to 30 years.

Moreover, all realistic scenarios indicate that many of the social and even governance indicators will remain unacceptable, or get worse, in the next few years, before they are made to improve.

It is important to focus, at least partially on how to live with these challenging scenarios, and alleviate them, before things improve. Banks, especially in the emerging markets where some of the worst ESG conditions now exist, can have an important role in managing the crises. Their efforts in these areas need also to be recognized and reflected economically, and even in the ratings they are given.

These ESG transition phases can be viewed as similar to the phases of the reaction to the COVID-19 pandemic. The world went through a "transition phase" before the solution eventually came with vaccines. The transition phase involved coping mechanisms. Similarly, the world will have to strengthen its coping mechanism on climate change through the transition phase. The "vaccine-equivalents" will come from several medium to long term measures – including technological innovations.

There is agreement among many that a "transition phase" into greener energy is the most workable path. Oil remains a very efficient source of energy. It is simply economically effective to use oil as long as possible, while reducing the Carbon impact of using it.

Moreover, very significant investments have been made in the oil industry across all countries. These investments are on the supply side; in oil production, pipelines, and refining. They are also on the "demand/

usage side" of oil. These include investments in oil-based transportation (ships, trucks, cars), manufacturing, and power generation. These large investments need to "run their course." Moreover, many new investments would be made (and have been made) in "transition" industries. Transition industries would continue to use oil, but would be more energy efficient. Examples of transition activities which would need transition investments and/or financing, include more efficient oil-fueled engines in manufacturing, transportation, hybrid cars, and replacement of shipping motors with more efficient ones.

Banks need to be involved in the ESG transition phases. These transitions can be summarized in their broad terms as a) transition in the energy mix from mainly fossil fuels, to mainly clean energy as the world moves closer to net zero, and b) managing the deteriorating situations in most countries in many social, and governance aspects, until things are made to improve.

8

ESG REPORTING AND DISCLOSURE METRICS

This chapter will discuss:

a. The importance of ESG reporting,
b. The principals for disclosure of ESG information that a bank, or company need to follow,
c. The ESG information that needs to be disclosed, i.e. what needs to be disclosed.

THE IMPORTANCE OF ESG REPORTING

BANKS AND COMPANIES EVERYWHERE, INCLUDING in the emerging markets, need to have ESG objectives and plans, implement them, and disclose these to their many stakeholders. This is because the stakeholders of banks and companies want to see that they are pursuing ESG goals. These stakeholders include investors, shareholders, clients, employees, suppliers, international financial institutions, rating agencies, and regulators.

The stakeholders of a bank, or a company, increasingly want environmental and other ESG factors to be taken into consideration in the activities of the bank they deal with. International investors, and large international banks would increasingly be asking, and expecting the companies and banks in the emerging markets to advise them on what they are doing about ESG goals. This is because investors and clearing banks are themselves being asked to report on what they are doing about ESG goals. The smaller banks are basically "clients" of the large international banks, and banks are expected to ensure their clients take into consideration the concerns of their stakeholders.

Companies and banks in Emerging Economies need to be seen as meeting measurable Environmental, Social and Governance targets, if they are to attract international investors. Banks and companies should not wait for the common ESG standards and measurements to be agreed upon. The goal is to move on, as large banks are doing. No organization will have perfect measurements and reporting for the first years of reporting. Doing a partial job is better than doing nothing.

Reporting on ESG is certainly necessary. The non-reporting of what a company, or a bank is doing on ESG would increasingly be seen as possible absence of any action (or interest) in ESG. It could be seen eventually as "non-compliant" when more ESG guidelines are issued by regulators.

Separate, stand-alone sustainability/ESG reports are also necessary. Some companies and banks now report on ESG in their annual reports, and this reporting tends to be perfunctory. Stand-alone ESG reports help bring focus on ESG issues.

This ESG reporting should also not be a one-size-fits-all. This is because some banks and companies have different business profiles, different sizes, and different impact on the economies they serve. Moreover, it is for each bank, company, and each country to determine their objectives in the ESG spheres, especially in Social and Governance spheres.

It should also be understood that reporting on ESG should include reporting on the progress of ESG implementation. ESG goals are themselves not short-term goals, and are expected to be achieved in the medium to long term. This applies to almost all elements of ESG. Net-zero emissions, for example, are expected to be achieved in 2050. Obviously any report on this goal is a progress report by the very nature of the activity being reported on. The same would apply to other goals, like gender equality. So whether a bank or a company is reporting on ESG activities for the first time, or in the fifth year, its reports are progress reports. This would also be progress reporting on the transition of ESG activities from basic ones to more comprehensive ones.

ESG reporting can be relatively simple in the initial year(s). The quality of ESG reporting would also be expected to improve with time. This would be the result of data becoming more available, and being accumulated over time. It would also benefit from common standards becoming more widely acceptable.

Banks and companies need to build their "internal capacity" to report on ESG, regardless of how they decide to report on ESG in the near future. A bank or company would find that it is far easier for it to disclose ESG information, if it had started building data at an earlier stage. This would facilitate both a) the disclosure process, and b) the verification process. Equally important, it would facilitate the management of ESG-related risks (especially climate risks).

THE PRINCIPLES FOR DISCLOSURE OF ESG INFORMATION

The principles for ESG disclosures that a bank can follow are very well defined by the Basel Committee in the Corporate Governance guidance. These disclosure principles can be followed by companies as well. We will now go over a number of the more important of these Basel disclosure principles. Moreover, we will go over the disclosure principles established by the TCFD – The Task Force for Climate-related Financial Disclosures. These two disclosure sources have "overlapping" principles, but it is worthwhile to list them both.

The Basel disclosure (and/or transparency) principles that would be relevant for ESG disclosures include the following points:

The governance of the bank should be adequately transparent to its shareholders, depositors, other relevant stakeholders and market participants.

*"(**Point 151**) Transparency is consistent with sound and effective corporate governance. As emphasised in existing Committee guidance on bank transparency, it is difficult for shareholders, depositors, other relevant stakeholders and market participants to effectively monitor and properly hold the board and senior management accountable when there is insufficient transparency. The objective of transparency in the area of corporate governance is therefore to provide these parties with the information necessary to enable them to assess the effectiveness of the board and senior management in governing the bank."*

*"(**Point 153**) All banks, even those for whom disclosure requirements may differ because they are non-listed, should disclose relevant and useful information that supports the key areas of corporate governance identified by the Committee. Such <u>disclosure should be proportionate to the size, complexity, structure, economic significance and risk profile of the bank</u>."*

*"(**Point 154**) In general, the bank should apply the disclosure and transparency section of the OECD principles. Accordingly, <u>disclosure should include</u>, but not be limited to, <u>material information</u> on the bank's objectives, organisational and governance structures and policies (in particular, the content of any corporate governance or remuneration code or policy and the process by which it is implemented). Measures that reflect the longer-term performance of the bank should also be presented."*

*"(**Point 155**) The bank should also disclose key points concerning its risk exposures and risk management strategies without breaching necessary confidentiality."*

*"(**Point 156**) Disclosure should be accurate, clear and presented such that shareholders, depositors, other relevant stakeholders and market participants can consult the information easily. Timely public disclosure is desirable on a bank's public website, in its annual and periodic financial reports, or by other appropriate means."*

The TCFD established "Fundamental Principles for Effective Disclosure." These are very well thought out principles, and can be adopted for disclosure in all ESG areas, not only those related to climate change. These principles are seven in number, but we have added an eighth point on verification, which is actually implied in point 6:

1. Disclosures should present relevant information,
2. Disclosures should be specific and complete,
3. Disclosures should be clear, balanced, and understandable,
4. Disclosures should be consistent over time,
5. Disclosures should be comparable among organizations within a sector, industry, or portfolio,
6. Disclosures should be reliable, verifiable, and objective,
7. Disclosures should be provided on a timely basis.
8. Disclosures should be verified both internally, and independently by a third party.

THE ESG INFORMATION THAT NEEDS TO BE DISCLOSED: THE ESG METRICS

The ESG metrics that need to be disclosed can be "chosen" from the list of metrics that will follow in this section. This list is broken down by the three ESG categories: Environmental, Social, and Governance goals. The information that can be disclosed under each category is based on the discussion we have made of each of these categories in previous chapters.

The choice of what metrics a bank or company needs to make depends on what this bank's ESG objectives are. In all cases, the chosen metrics (and objectives) should be "material" (as the Basel Committee implies). The materiality is defined differently by different standard setters.

Materiality determination should include two main factors and objectives in our view:

a. There should be a "<u>need</u>" for the objective to be made. The need is determined by the different stakeholders of the bank or company. These stakeholders include, as mentioned earlier, investors, shareholders, clients, employees, suppliers, international financial institutions, rating agencies, and regulators.
Some of the chosen objectives would include ones that are needed on a "macro level," as they are material to the economy and/or country the bank or company works in. Climate change, and water scarcity are two good examples of ESG objectives where the needs are likely to be very stark in some countries or communities a bank or company serves.

Some of these needed objectives could be defined by the regulators. The example of a regulatory "material" objective is financial inclusion – where this objective is defined as material by many regulators in the emerging markets. It is necessary to add therefore that the regulators may have a major say in determining materiality of certain objectives for banks.

b. The "<u>impact</u>" of the work that a bank or company carries out, or finance, should be material in meeting an objective it sets for itself. In other words, what a bank or a company can achieve (by itself, or through finance) relative to its capabilities should be material to meet the objective it sets.

Following are the metrics that need to be disclosed in each of ESG goals. These are almost all a repetition of indicators already pointed out in earlier chapters. We repeat these here in one place, but in abridged format, for easy quick reference. The indicators to be reported are organized under the different categories of Environmental, Social and Governance goals. The indicators to be reported are highlighted in "points."

REPORTING ENVIRONMENTAL GOALS: CLIMATE CHANGE

Calculating and Offsetting the Carbon Footprint

The "climate change" objective of a bank or company is to <u>reach carbon neutrality</u>. To reach carbon neutrality, an entity (a company or a bank) should first a) calculate its carbon equivalent emissions. This is called the Carbon Footprint, which is total greenhouse gas emissions by a person, organization, event, or product. The company/bank should then b) put a plan to reduce these emissions, and/or purchase or finance carbon negative activities (or carbon credits). There are several standards to measure carbon neutrality. One of the better ones is PAS 2060, the carbon neutral standard developed by BSI (the British Standards Institute).

- <u>A bank or company should calculate its Carbon Footprint:</u>
  A company, or a bank, in an emerging country should aim to report Scope 1, Scope 2 and Scope 3 GHG emissions as defined in the chapter on Environmental Goals. This is measured by metric tons carbon dioxide equivalent as described earlier in this chapter.

- <u>A bank should calculate the Carbon Footprint from financial activities:</u>
  This involves the calculation of the GHG emitted by activities financed by the bank. This is the equivalent of Scope 3 emissions.

Banks, including in the emerging markets, would find that the Scope 3 emissions of their clients are significant, especially compared to the bank's own emissions. They would need accordingly to try to measure them and/or have their clients measure them. They would then need them to be disclosed.

There is no need to report Scope 3 emissions at initial stages/ years of reporting (mainly because of the difficulty of collecting data). However, Scope 3 emissions of banks (reflected mainly in loans) would likely become a major area of GHG measurement and disclosure of their emissions in the next few years. The sooner banks can start collecting data on these emissions, the easier it would be to disclose them in later years.

There are several efforts to address this issue, and among these is the "standard" issued in early 2021 by the PCAF (Partnership for Carbon Accounting Financials). The PCAF has developed GHG accounts and reporting standards of Scope 3 emissions particularly for the financial industry. It provides guidelines to measure (and then disclose) GHG emissions associated with six asset classes. These are a) listed equity and corporate bonds, b) business loans and unlisted equity, c) project finance, d) commercial real estate, e) mortgages, and f) motor vehicle loans.

Companies, and banks and financial institutions can work on addressing GHG emissions in different ways according to the activities they are involved in, or finance.

- Carbon Offsets can be reported:
  Offsets can be used to "neutralize" Scope 1 and 2 emissions. Some argue that offsets can be used to neutralize Scope 3 emissions as well (but only for a company/bank, but not a country).

Banks and companies can set up "carbon offset" programs for themselves. These programs would involve the offsetting of carbon emissions by those who have carbon emission activities. Banks would do that by purchasing "carbon credits," or carbon offsets that would result in their achieving net zero, or net reduction of their emissions.

Carbon offsets are "purchased" in units of metric tons of carbon dioxide, or carbon dioxide equivalent. Carbon offsets are brought about, according to the GHG Protocol from "activities intended to reduce GHG emissions, increase the storage of carbon, or enhance GHG removals from the atmosphere."

Working to Achieve a New Energy Mix, and Net Zero

As discussed in the chapter on "Environmental Goals: Climate Change," all those involved in the energy-planning process expect a far more diverse energy mix in 2050 than is the case today. Banks and companies need to work towards achieving the new energy mix, and report on these steps. They can work to achieve this energy mix themselves, and/or, more importantly, finance activities to reach it.

The indicators to be reported are the generally agreed key steps that need to be taken to achieve a new energy mix, and ultimately net zero. These would include:

- Behavior and avoided demand of energy: These include efforts to limit the usage to the extent possible.
- Energy Efficiency: Efforts to improve energy efficiencies, especially where fossil fuels need to be used. An example of better fossil fuel efficiency is the improvement of fuel efficiency of aeroplanes.
- Move to the more carbon-efficient fossil fuels. These are a) natural gas, then b) petroleum, then c) coal, in that order. Coal would be phased out.
- Electrification increases, and efficiencies in electric power generation. These would also include the increase in battery-powered engines, and battery storage capacities.
- Renewable and clean energy. Energy from "clean" sources will have to continue to increase exponentially and increase their share in the energy "mix." Renewable energy sources would come mostly from solar power. Other sources would be wind, hydrogen, geothermal, bioenergy, and nuclear energy.

- Support to technological improvements needed to achieve net zero.
- Support of more digitization which is "environmentally-friendly." This includes the example of working from home.
- Financing of activities to achieve net zero. These are mainly the activities mentioned above. Financing these measures is the most important role of a bank, especially in the emerging markets.

Working to achieve, and finance Carbon Capture, Utilization, and Storage: CCUS

Carbon capture utilization and storage (CCUS) would allow for the partial reduction of carbon present in the atmosphere because of emissions from fossil fuels.

The metrics that can be used to measure CCUS can be:
- Carbon dioxide and other GHGs captured and utilized, or stored by the bank,
- Financing of companies that are involved in CCS, or CCU.
- Support to permanent forestation and agriculture.

Getting Involved in, and Developing Carbon Markets:

Carbon markets can serve to intermediate between those who have GHG emissions (and therefore demand carbon credits), and those who supply carbon credits. These credits are created by activities that a) avoid, b) reduce, and/or c) capture and remove carbon through usage or storage (CCUS). This transaction is generally called carbon-offset.

- Banks can report on their general support to, and involvement in, carbon markets. Banks can report on any intermediating activity they have in the carbon markets.
- Banks can report on how many carbon credits they helped create through financing of carbon credit creating projects.

- Banks can also play a role in intermediating carbon credits buy/ sell transactions, whether these transactions are inter-country, or intra-country.

REPORTING ENVIRONMENTAL GOALS: THE ECOSYSTEM

Water Scarcity and Sanitation

The reporting on water is necessary especially in high-water-stress countries. The World Resources Institute (WRI) gives a rating of water stress levels for most countries of the world. There are five WRI water stress categories: Extremely High, High, Medium-High, Low-Medium, and Low.

The main water metric is well covered by the Sustainability Accounting Standards Board. However, a bank does not need to go into detail on water management. A bank's reporting details should depend on its relative size, as per the proportionality principle.

The reporting on water scarcity, and sanitation can include:

- Banks and companies in countries in the first 3 water-stress category countries should report on their consumption of water when they start reporting on ESG. In later years, they can measure and report on water consumption of their clients as well.
- Banks should report on their efforts to increase the supply of fresh water, including their financing of these activities.
- Any initiative that a bank or company might have to increase water cleanliness can be reported. This relates to the second part of SDG number 6.
- Banks or companies can also report on any water initiative they have, support, or finance. These initiatives would be to reduce water consumption and withdrawal, or increase the supply of fresh water. These initiatives can be profitable if water is priced correctly. This pricing could be up to governments to determine in many countries.

Water Desalination

- A bank may report on its financing of desalination plants, large or small, as a positive contribution to ESG.
- A bank can report on its issuance of, or subscription in, Blue bonds and Desalination bonds. The proceeds from these bonds are mainly aimed at reaching SDG goal number 14.

Plastics and the Seas

Banks and companies can report on their <u>participating directly in, or financing of</u>, one or more activities to control plastic pollution. These include, as mentioned in an earlier chapter:

- Using and/or financing alternatives to plastics,
- Putting limits on the use of single-use plastics,
- Eliminating unnecessary packaging,
- Transitioning to return-and-reuse systems,
- Substituting virgin with recycled plastic or switching to other materials like paper,
- Capturing plastic waste effectively. This includes plastics on land and sea,
- Disposing of plastic waste,
- Recycling of plastic waste

Air Quality Measurements

- A bank or company should monitor and report both indoor and outdoor air pollution, but focus more on indoor air pollutants – which are under its control. The idea of tracking only outside air pollution, as some standard setters do, is not the most effective methodology in our view. Both should be measured, and disclosed/reported, and tackled.

  There are several readily available instruments that can measure the pollutants commonly regarded as most harmful.

Measurements of air pollution must be made, and if they have not been started, they need to be. An extensive listing of the most common air pollutants have been given in a separate section in the chapter on Environmental Goals: The Ecosystem. <u>The main air pollutants that need to be measured indoors are the following</u>:

- PM2.5: Inhalable Particulate Matter
- PM10: Particulate matter that are larger than 2.5 micrometers, but less than 10 micrometers
- CO2: Carbon Dioxide
- TVOC: Total Volatile Organic Compounds
- Radon

Waste Management

- Banks and companies need to report on their efforts to manage the waste they generate. These efforts need to be in an environmentally friendly manner.
- Banks need to report on their financing of their clients who are involved in waste management or who specialize in waste management.
- Banks and companies can report on their involvement in the design and implementation of the circular economy.

REPORTING SOCIAL GOALS

The detailed metrics that can be reported on social goals in each category:

ESG: Gender Equality

This goal conforms with SDG 5. The metrics that banks and companies can report on, and can use to measure and ensure gender equality can be:

- Percentage of females in the bank or company workforce.
- Women as a percentage in senior positions.
- Number of females and males recruited and/or promoted, to executive and non-executive positions in the last year.
- Average pay of females vs. average pay of males.
- Percentage of females attending training during a year, compared to percentage of females in the work force.
- Percentage of female clients (individual/retail) or women as a percentage of account holders.
- Percentage of customer businesses controlled and/or owned by women.
- Loans to women, or businesses controlled and/or owned, by women.
- Women as a percentage of financial inclusion drives.
- Performance Indicators (KPI's) on Gender equality for CEO, and senior executives.
- Any independent "sounding" of staff needs to include the ability of females for advancement in the bank.

Financial Inclusion, and Financial Literacy

This conforms with SDGs 8, 1, and 2. The metrics that banks can use to measure financial inclusion, and financial literacy, include:

- Number of new accounts opened to individuals in lower income groups, and small businesses.
- Number of products used by accounts of individuals in lower income groups, and small businesses (i.e. cross-selling of products).

- Number of new accounts opened to women, especially women in lower income groups.
- Efforts to improve financial knowledge. This is especially important because "financial education" is proven to increase financial inclusion.

Financial Education/Training

This conforms with SDG 4. The metrics that banks and companies can use to measure this needed education and training goal can include:

- Percentage of staff trained per year,
- Hours of training per staff per year,
- Financial investment/cost of training,
- Investment in training compared to overall expense (or staff expenses),
- Support for professional certifications of staff, such as in compliance,
- In-house training and outside training by hours and cost,
- E-training and classroom training breakdowns, and
- Support for, or financing of, education institutions, and students.

Consumer Protection

A bank or company needs to report on its consumer protection framework and efforts. The metrics that can be used by a bank to measure this consumer-protection "social goal" follow. Some of these general consumer protection requirements overlap with Governance requirements, and some standard-setters actually include them under "governance" requirements:

- Existence of systems to protect consumers,
- Existence of complaint mechanisms for customers,
- Implementation of systems to protect the privacy of customers and their data,

- Implementation of cybersecurity systems to protect all stake-holders of a bank,
- Implementation of systems to protect against fraud,
- Implementation of processes to protect against money laundering,
- Implementation of processes to protect against financing of terrorism.

ESG - Health

This conforms with SDG 3. The main health indicators a company or bank should have or finance are mostly the following ones.

- A bank or company should report on health coverage of its employees.
- A bank or company should report whether health coverage is comprehensive. Comprehensive health coverage covers all hospitalization costs – with the possibility that an employee must contribute a percentage of the cost. This should ideally not exceed 10%. Comprehensive coverage can also include dental and eye coverage, maternity leave and child care facilities.
- The company or bank should report whether it has a health regime that has "preventive health." The areas covered by preventive health include regular check-ups.
- A bank or company can report on "the second stage" of health coverage. This has banks reporting on "occupational hazards" in their lending activities. It is sometimes crucial in some industries to ensure the borrower has proper coverage for its employees. Those industries include construction companies, and chemical plants.
- The organization/bank can report on efforts to ensure a healthy work-life balance for its staff. This balance is important for both the mental and physical health of employees.
- The organization/bank needs to measure and report on absentee rates of employees to see whether there are health issues.

- The company or bank should report on efforts to inform employees that mental well-being is as important as physical health.
- There should be reporting on working hours of employees. Excessive working hours have been shown to be counter-productive, and affect the physical and mental health of employees.

Pay Equality

This conforms with SDG 10. Banks and companies need to report on their efforts to achieve pay equality for their employees. They also need to ask their clients about their efforts in this area. Companies and banks need to avoid dealing with clients with glaring pay equality gaps.

Privacy

Companies and banks need to report on their efforts to protect the privacy of their clients. It should also involve reporting on the cybersecurity systems to protect them. There are extensive sources dealing with privacy and cybersecurity requirements, and we will therefore not cover them in detail here.

Community Support

A bank or company needs to report on its community support. There are significant overlaps between the "older" CSR reporting, the Corporate Social Responsibility, and Social Goals reporting of ESG. These need not be reported twice. A bank or company can simply incorporate its CSR reporting into its ESG reporting in the "Social" pillar.

Ethical Operations

A company or bank needs to ensure its operations are ethical. It also needs to ensure that suppliers have ethical practices. This can be a significant issue with suppliers from some developing countries. Financial needs might lead some suppliers to have certain practices not acceptable elsewhere – such as child labor.

Assessment of the ESG Practices of Customers and Suppliers (the supply chain)

A company or a bank needs to report on the ESG practices of its main suppliers, to the extent this might be material.

REPORTING GOVERNANCE GOALS

Governance, the third pillar of ESG, is important for the same reasons that make it important to pursue environmental and social goals, the other two pillars of ESG. The first reason is that there is a major need to have good governance, and the second is that there would be a high impact from very strong governance on achieving ESG goals.

Governance in ESG covers two interrelated domains. The first is governance of ESG management itself.

Governance of ESG is mainly about developing principles and practices for the governance and oversight of the environmental, and social, elements of ESG. These principles and practices have been developed by many standard setters. However, there are no generally acceptable standards for ESG governance, as is the case with the other standards covering ESG. Amdeya has developed a comprehensive set of principles and practices for governance of ESG in banks.

The second set of governance requirements of ESG for a bank or company are the general corporate governance requirements. The foundational documents for corporate governance for banks in the emerging countries is the "Guidelines on Corporate Governance" issued by the Basel Committee on Banking Supervision.

Reports on Governance goals in both domains (ESG Governance, and Corporate Governance) would include:

- Business strategy
- Tone from the top

- Board composition
- Board organization
- Performance evaluations
- Disclosure
- Verification
- ESG Planning
- Risk Management
- Materiality Assessment
- Application of the Proportionality Principle
- Board training
- Code of Business Conduct
- Supply Chain Management
- Digital Security
- Data Security

www.ingramcontent.com/pod-product-compliance
Lightning Source LLC
Chambersburg PA
CBHW021414210526
45463CB00001B/361